Mismanaging Innovation Systems

T0298371

Once recognised as a high-performing newly industrialising Asian economy with the potential for economic and developmental success similar to South Korea, Taiwan, Hong Kong and Singapore, Thailand's growth rate and competitive edge have declined substantially. With slower adoption and movement towards knowledge-intensive industries, the loss of the competitive edge is a cause of growing concern among Thai policymakers, with Thailand succumbing to the middle-income trap. This book analyses Thailand's declining competitiveness in the past 50 years, considering both the national and sectoral roles and capabilities of key players, including government, universities and research institutes, as well as the electronics, food, and automotive industries.

Including comparative analyses with other Asian nations, this book is a must-read for both students and practitioners with interests in development economics, industrial economics and public policy.

Patarapong Intarakumnerd is Professor at the National Graduate Institute for Policy Studies (GRIPS) in Tokyo, Japan. He is a regional editor and member of international editorial boards of several international journals relating to innovation management and policies. He has worked as an advisor/consultant for the World Bank, UNESCO, UNCTAD, OECD, Japan International Cooperation Agency (JICA), German Development Institute, International Development Research Center of Canada, and the Economic Research Institute of ASEAN and East Asia (ERIA).

Routledge-GRIPS Development Forum Studies
Edited by Kenichi Ohno and Izumi Ohno
National Graduate Institute for Policy Studies, Japan

For a full list of titles in this series, visit www.routledge.com/Routledge-GRIPS-Development-Forum-Studies/book-series/GRIPS

Mismanaging Innovation Systems
Thailand and the Middle-income Trap

Patarapong Intarakumnerd

Routledge
Taylor & Francis Group

LONDON AND NEW YORK

First published 2018
by Routledge

2 Park Square, Milton Park, Abingdon, Oxfordshire OX14 4RN
52 Vanderbilt Avenue, New York, NY 10017

Routledge is an imprint of the Taylor & Francis Group, an informa business

First issued in paperback 2019

British Library Cataloguing-in-Publication Data
A catalogue record for this book is available from the British Library

Library of Congress Cataloging-in-Publication Data
A catalog record for this book has been requested

ISBN: 978-1-138-12482-0 (hbk)
ISBN: 978-0-367-37481-5 (pbk)

Typeset in Galliard
by Apex CoVantage, LLC

This book is dedicated to my parents (Tanom and Raewadee) and my grandparents (Saroh and Praipun) for their love and kindness

Contents

Tables

Preface

What has gone wrong in Thailand? The country was once recognised as a high-performing newly industrialising economy (NIE) which could be successful in industrial catch-up with the West, similar to what Korea, Taiwan, Hong Kong and Singapore had previously done. Now the new normal growth rate is only about 2–3 per cent per year. The middle-income trap became the talk to the town. We analyse Thailand's declining competitiveness through the evolution of innovation systems in the past 50 years. At the national level, we investigate the roles, capabilities and interactions of key actors, namely, government, firms, universities, public research institutes, industrial and professional associations and financial intermediaries. We also shed light on the role of institutional factors (entrepreneurship, policymaker mindsets, and intellectual property rights) in shaping the technological learning and innovation of firms. Finally, we examine innovation systems in key sectors, namely electronics, seafood and automotive.

Acknowledgements

This study was supported by JSPS KAKENHI [grant number 25101006]. I would like to express my gratitude to Prof. Tetsushi Sonobe, the leader of the Emerging State Project, and Prof. Keiichi Tsunekawa, the group leader, for their kind support and leadership.

Abbreviations

ACFS	National Bureau of Agricultural Commodity and Food Standards
BIOTEC	National Biotechnology Centre
BOI	board of investment
CBU	completely build unit
CEOs	chief executive officers
CKD	completely knock down
DIP	Department of Intellectual Property
EDB	Economic Development Board (Singapore)
EEC	Eastern economic corridor
EEI	Electrical and Electronics Institute
EMS	electronics manufacturing services
FDA	Food and Drug Administration (Thailand)
FDI	foreign direct investment
FEPS	Food Engineering Practice School
FoSTAT	Food Science and Technology Association of Thailand
FTI	Federation of Thai Industries
GDP	gross domestic product
GERD	gross expenditure on research and development
GMP	good manufacturing practice
HACCP	hazard analysis and critical control point
HDD	hard disk drive
HDDI	hard disk drive institute
IC	integrated circuit
ICT	information and communications technology
IDEMA	International Disk Drive Equipment and Materials Association
IP&IT	Intellectual Property and International Trade Court
IPC	Intellectual Property Centre
IPRs	intellectual property rights
ITAP	Industrial Technology Assistance Programme
JPPCC	joint public–private consultative committee
KIPI	Korea Institute of Patent Information
KMITL	King Mongkut's Institute of Technology, Ladkrabang
KMUTNB	King Mongkut's University of Technology, North Bangkok

KMUTT	King Mongkut's University of Technology, Thonburi
M&A	merger and acquisition
MMA	microelectronics module assembly
MU	Mahidol University
NECTEC	National Electronics and Computer Technology Centre
NESDB	National Economic and Social Development Board
NFI	National Food Institute
NIA	National Innovation Agency
NIEs	newly industrialising economies
NRCT	National Research Council of Thailand
NRIC	National Research and Innovation Policy Council
NSTDA	National Science and Technology Development Agency
OBM	own brand manufacturer
ODM	own design manufacturer
OEM	original equipment Manufacturer
R&D	research and development
RFID	radio frequency identification
S&T	science and technology
SMEs	small and medium enterprises
SPRING	Standards, Productivity and Innovation Board (Singapore)
STI	science, technology and innovation
SGD	Singapore dollar
TAI	Thailand Automotive Institute
TAPMA	Thai Auto Parts Manufacturers Association
TCC	Thai Chamber of Commerce
TESA	Thailand Embedded Systems Association
TFP	total factor productivity
TFFA	Thai Frozen Foods Association
THB	Thai Baht
TMC	Technology Management Centre
TMEC	Thai Microelectronic Centre
TNCs	transnational corporations
TNI	Thai–Nichi Institute of Technology
TPA	Technology Promotion Association (Thailand–Japan)
TRF	Thailand research fund
TRIPS	trade-related aspects of intellectual property rights
TTCAP	Toyota Technical Centre Asia Pacific
TWD	Taiwan dollar
UILs	university–industry linkages
VC	venture capital
VLSI	very large scale integration
WTO	World Trade Organisation

1 Introduction

During the mid-1980s and mid-1990s, Thailand was recognised as a high-performing newly industrialising economy (NIE) which could catch-up to industry in the West, similar to what Korea, Taiwan, Hong Kong and Singapore had done before. The country experienced double-digit growth of gross domestic product (GDP) and was able to diversify its economy with various agriculture and manufacturing products and thriving services, especially tourism. Nonetheless, the country faced a major economic crisis in 1997. Although the economic situation improved within a few years afterwards, the country's long-term growth rate and competitiveness in once-rising-star and labour-intensive products like textiles, shoes and clothing declined substantially. At the same time, the country failed to climb the technological ladder to produce more knowledge-intensive products and services. These circumstances caused growing concerns among Thai policymakers and more recently, the general public, that Thailand is about to be in the *middle-income trap*,[1] because the country has had upper middle-income levels for 14 years in 2017.

What went wrong with Thailand? We analyse Thailand's declining competitiveness through the evolution of innovation systems in the past 50 years. At a national level, we investigate the roles, capabilities and interactions of key actors, namely, government, firms (transnational corporations, large Thai firms, SMEs, and start-ups), universities, public research institutes, industrial and professional associations and financial intermediaries (banks, venture capitals and capital market). This book also sheds light on the role of institutional factors (such as entrepreneurship, policymaker mindsets, intellectual property rights, and trust) in shaping the technological learning and innovation of firms in Thailand. In addition to analysis at the national level, we examine innovation systems in the key sectors of electronics, food and automotive industries.

The primary objective of this book is to analyse why a promising Asian power like Thailand is now losing its competitive advantages and stuck in the middle-income trap. This is an interesting question to scholars, policymakers and those with an interest in economic development and industrialisation.

The book offers an innovative way to analyse technological and economic pursuit of a late-industrialising country with four points:

1 By adopting the concept of innovation system, the book provides a *holistic, longitudinal and historically friendly* analysis and synthesis of Thailand's

industrialisation and technological development in the past 50 years. This differs from previous studies that focused on a specific and a snapshot aspect of industrial development. We examine key actors in innovation systems, how they interact and learn together, and the roles of shaping institutions, like law, regulations, norms, entrepreneurship, intellectual property rights and others.

2   The book analyses innovation systems at the national level. It also evaluates development at the sectoral level and attempts to link these two levels together. Technological development of a sector depends on circumstances at both the national and the sectoral levels. The sectors evaluated here are a high-tech industry (electronics), a mid-tech industry (automotive), and a resource-based industry (food).

3   Though the book concentrates on Thailand, it also compares the national level policies of Thailand with more successful industrialised Asian countries, like Japan, Korea, Taiwan and Singapore. At the sector level, we also consider relevant experiences of other countries.

4   The book focuses on policy and action, rather than offering a theoretical breakthrough. By examining the behaviours and underlying capabilities of various actors, how they work collectively and institutions supporting and obstructing the learning processes, it presents a straightforward understanding of the current situation in Thailand.

1.1   Overview of Thailand's economic development since 1950s

In the past 50 years, Thailand has achieved consistently high GDP growth rates, approximately 7 per cent per annum, and significantly diversified its economy. Industrialisation in Thailand can be divided into three periods: import substitution (late 1950s–1970s), export promotion (1980s–mid-1990s) and liberalisation (late 1990s onwards). The contribution of the agriculture sector to GDP was significantly reduced from 44 per cent in 1951 to 8.7 per cent in 2015, while the share of manufacturing markedly increased from 13 per cent to 27.5 per cent in the same period. Nonetheless, in terms of export, while the role of primary products has declined relative to that of manufacturing, agriculture has been diversified significantly, as Thailand has become one of the world's top exporters of a wide range of primary or primary-based products, including rice, rubber, sugar, cassava and also prawns and canned pineapple. At the same time, the growth and diversification of manufactured exports, in sectors from textiles, automobiles and parts and electronic and electrical components, has also been impressive. For example, the shares of exports of electronic and automotive products, respectively, increased from 0.04 and 0.25 in the year 1970 to 25.20 and 6.68 in the year 2006 respectively (Yusuf and Nabeshima, 2009). Thailand's economic status changed from that of a low-income country to an upper middle-income country by 2003. Behind this success lies prudent macroeconomic management, early adoption of export and foreign direct investment promotion policies, investment in physical infrastructure, and the expansion of school and university enrolment (World Bank, 1993).

Nonetheless, some scholars, such as Yoshihara Kunio (1988), strongly questioned the sustainability of Thailand's economic prosperity. He describes the Thai economy as 'Ersatz Capitalism'. Unlike Western countries, Japan and other first-tier East Asian NIEs, the Thai economy grew by overcoming bottlenecks with foreign technology and capital without making serious efforts to increase its own saving and upgrade technology. He believes that this type of capitalism cannot keep expanding. Kunio's prediction came true. The country experienced a major economic crisis in 1997. Since then, the economic growth rates have decreased substantially, to 3–4 per cent annually, and they decreased even further, to 2–3 per cent on average after 2014, when the military took over the country. This growth rate has become the new normal for Thailand. The country's once-rising-star and labour-intensive sectors, like textiles, clothing, toys and shoes, have lost their competitive edge to countries paying lower wages. The concern about middle-income trap is widespread among Thai policymakers, scholars and the public. More specifically, there is concern about the limited intensity of technology development in industry which has contributed to that competitive weakness. This has been reflected in a number of key economic indicators, especially the growth of total factor productivity (TFP). TFP's growth indicates other contributors to a country's economic growth beyond that of capital, labour and land. Apart from education and other social capital and institutional factors, it includes the progress of science and technology and innovation. Although Thailand's economic growth rate in the past 50 years is rather impressive, this has been achieved largely by utilising factor inputs. Between 1987–1995, the Thai economy grew at the rate almost 10 per cent, and the TFP growth rate was only around 1.5 per cent (NESDB, 2007a).

1.2   Middle-income trap

The term "middle-income trap" (henceforth, MIT) is a relatively new phrase invented by Gill and Kharas in their *East Asian Renaissance* report (2007). However, it is appealing and perhaps ambiguous enough to become a powerful buzzword in the international development community within a short period of time. Whether or not a country has a "middle-income" level depends on the definition provided by the World Bank.[2] But the debate over the "trap" is another matter. Despite using the same phrase, the MIT literature varies considerably in the cases studied, the research methods employed, the underlying causes of the trap, and the policies suggested.

There are three schools of thoughts to explain why countries are in the MIT.

A.   *Getting education and institutions right*

Studies in this group analyse middle-income countries, with special reference to the quality of education and institutions. For example, Jimenez et al. (2012,

p. 16) explore Thailand and Malaysia compared to Korea, and they argue that human capital formation is fundamental to sustaining per capita income growth, as it equips workers with marketable skills. The list of MIT problems in Jitsuchon (2012, p. 16) is longer and summarised as "Thailand's institutional weaknesses". In addition to poor educational quality, an incomplete market in skills training, a low level of research and development (R&D) activities and spending, and flawed tax structure are included. A more comprehensive study of probit regressions covering 138 countries from 1955 to 2009 was conducted by Aiyar et al. (2013). High-quality institutions – defined as: strong rule of law; small government; and light regulation – are among significant factors contributing to change in growth, and slowdowns, of middle-income countries.

As for policy suggestions, Jitsuchon (2012, p. 19) proposes that the Thai government should not interfere with the market but should "devise the right incentive system so that economic agents would want to pursue their own prosperity . . . Providing public research infrastructure and tax benefits for implementing innovation and R&D activities is an example". For Aiyar et al. (2013, p. 32), reforms should cover "prudential regulation to limit the build-up of excessive capital inflows . . . measures to enhance regional trade integration, public investment in infrastructure projects, and deregulation in areas where red tape is stifling private activity". In short, the state should generate the best incentive systems and invest more in education, institutions, and R&D.

B.   *Changing export composition by following comparative advantage*

Rather than education and institutions, the second school of thought points to a country's export composition as critical to the success or failure of pursuit. Some studies in this group draw underlying theory from 'old-school' development economics.

Felipe et al. (2012, p. 33) argue that development and growth should be seen as "a process of structural transformation of the productive structure, whereby resources were transferred from activities of lower productivity into activities of higher productivity". Using a data set with 124 countries from 1950 to 2010, they found that products have different consequences for economic development. Successful catch-up occurs in countries with a "diversified, sophisticated, and non-standard level export basket". For example, while Korea was able to gain comparative advantage in a significant number of sophisticated products, Malaysia and the Philippines were only able to gain comparative advantage in electronics. Specific to Latin American and the Caribbean countries, Lin and Treichel (2012) argue that they have been caught in the MIT because of their inability to upgrade from low to high value-added production. Although not following the above underlying theory, the econometric findings in Eichengreen et al. (2013, pp. 11–12) also emphasise the importance of export compositions, among other contributing factors: "Countries accumulating high quality human capital and moving into the production of higher tech exports stand a better chance of avoiding the middle income trap".

Policy suggestions vary in this group, but they generally prefer the state to function as a facilitator who supports a country's transformation towards higher value-added exports. For example, Lin and Treichel (2012) assert that the govern-ment should play a crucial role in helping firms overcome information, coordination and externality problems. Elsewhere, Lin (2012, p. 397) clearly proposes that: "The best way for a developing country to achieve sustained, dynamic growth is to follow comparative advantage in its industrial development and to tap into the potential of advantages of backwardness in industrial upgrading".

C.   *Industrial upgrading by the proactive state*

Similar to the second group, this body of literature emphasises exports and production structures. Nevertheless, it explicitly supports the role of the state in acquiring indigenous technology for latecomers. For example, Ohno (2009) maps out four stages of catch-up industrialisation: (1) having simple manu-facturing under foreign guidance; (2) developing supporting industries but keeping production under foreign management; (3) internalising skills and knowledge by accumulating industrial human capital; and (4) acquiring the capabilities to create new products and lead global market trends. The MIT is defined as the "glass ceiling" between the second and third stages. Proactive industrial policy, with a strong commitment to global integration and private sector driven growth, is accorded the key role in solving the problem (Ohno, 2009, pp. 29–30).

Considering the perspectives of small countries,[3] the special issue on the MIT in *Studies in Comparative International Development* emphasises the competitive squeeze from the low and the high-end, highlighting the intense pressures on middle-income countries in the current globalisation process. Therein, Paus (2012, p. 130) demonstrates that: "Sustained broad-based upgrading happens where there is a proactive government with an overall focus on capability accumulation and deliberate attention to advancing social capabilities in sync with the needs of private sector upgrading."

1.3   National and sectoral innovation system concepts and outline of the book

Unlike the three schools of thoughts, this book will illustrate that Thailand's MIT is caused by failures of the country's innovation systems in technological learning and industrial upgrading. The book is divided into two parts. Part 1 focuses on the analysis of national innovation systems, that is, key actors, their interaction and collective learning, and influential institutional factors. Part 2 deeply investigates the innovation systems of Thailand's strategic industrial sectors, namely, the electronics, automotive and food industries.

Part I: Thailand's national innovation system: performance of key actors

The *national innovation system* is an interactive system of existing institutions, private and public firms (either large or small), universities and government agencies, that produce knowledge within national borders. Interaction among these units may be technical, commercial, legal, social and financial, as the goals of interactions may be the development, protection, financing, or regulation of new knowledge (Niosi et al., 1993).

We will use this concept to analyse the technological and industrial development of Thailand from Chapter 2 to Chapter 6.

Chapter 2: Science, technology and innovation policy of the Thai government

The chapter examines policy content, formulation and implementation processes in the past 50 years, until the military took over the government in 2014. It highlights that despite some changes in policy content and processes, Thailand's STI policies were static. These circumstances are very different from East Asian countries like Korea, Taiwan and Singapore, which are more successful with technological catch-up. The Thai government emphasised the R&D capabilities of firms, while neglecting other important capabilities for catch-up, namely. design and engineering. It perceived that firms were the *users* of STI capabilities generated by universities and public research institutes. Building indigenous technological and innovative capabilities within firms was *not* a major economic policy objective. Selective policies for particular sectors or clusters were rare, as they were considered as market distortions. Policies to promote technological upgrades to transnational corporations (TNCs) and local technological spillover were adequately implemented later. Government grants and direct subsidies to promote firms' technological learning have been limited. Creating a postgraduate science and technology workforce was prioritised over vocational education.

Chapter 3: Technological learning and innovation of firms in Thailand

The chapter explores the development of technological capabilities in various types of firms: TNCs, large domestic firms, small and medium enterprises and start-up companies. It compares these firms with those in East Asian economies (Taiwan, Korea, and Singapore) by analysing national innovation surveys and previous studies by the author and others. Firms in Thailand are much more passive with regard to technological learning. However, the situation has changed after the financial crisis in 1997, which was a stimulus for many large domestic firms, subcontractors of TNCs and start-up companies.

Chapter 4: Universities and public research institutes

Universities and public research institutes are perceived as much more important in driving the economy at present. Their teaching and research activities are more relevant to industry and society. They are expected to directly contribute to the emergence and growth of entrepreneurs and enterprises. We investigate the historical development of Thai universities and public research institutes and their impacts on human resource and enterprise development. Specifically, we assess how and to what extent universities and public research institutes in Thailand could contribute to the technological learning processes of firms. Through existing surveys and case studies, we found that collaborative research and training were the preferred mode of interaction with the industry, rather than the licensing of intellectual property rights and human mobility. Unlike more advanced Asian economies, universities collaborated more with firms in resource-based industries than those in science-based industries.

Chapter 5: Innovation financing

Instruments for innovation financing in Thailand have primarily been limited to tax incentives for R&D activities. In the more successful catch-up economies, like Taiwan, Singapore and Malaysia, grants and public equity financing have been extensively used to finance activities ranging from starting new companies, implementing new production technologies, engineering, design, R&D, R&D commercialisation, marketing and branding. Compared to Taiwan and Singapore, private venture capital in Thailand invested more in firms in the rapid-growth phase than in the start-up and early-growth phases. Private business angels investing in start-up firms were quite few compared to those countries.

Chapter 6: Institutions

The technological learning of firms has been influenced by several institutional factors which were very difficult to change. From innovation surveys, the attitudes towards risk-taking and accepting failure were rather negative, though they have improved overtime. In addition, from more recent global entrepreneurship surveys, Thais ranked very highly in their willingness to start new businesses. As most capitalists in Thailand have been overseas Chinese, the Chinese innovation management style is analysed. In addition to private firms, we elucidate the attitude of policymakers, especially technocrats in economic development and science and technology development spheres. Their attitudes were different from those in other East Asian countries, resulting to differences in policy contents and implementation. The important issues of changing intellectual property rights were highlighted. Again, the Thai case is different from those of more advanced East Asian countries, leading to different impacts of firms' technological learning.

Part II: Sectoral innovation systems of strategic industries

The *sectoral innovation system concept* was developed by an evolutionary economist, Franco Malerba. The framework focuses on the nature, structure, organisation and dynamics of innovation and production in sectors. Based on evolutionary theory and the innovation system approach, he defines a sector as a set of activities that are unified by some linked product groups for a given or emerging demand that share some common knowledge. Firms in a sector have some

8 *Introduction*

commonalities, and they are heterogeneous, in terms of learning processes and capabilities. The key elements in a sectoral system of innovation are:

1 *Firms in the sector.*
2 *Other actors.* These can be organisations or individuals. Organisations may be suppliers, users, universities, financial institutions, government agencies, trade unions or technical associations. Individuals may be consumers, entrepreneurs or scientists.
3 *Networks.* Firms are connected in various ways through *market and non-market relationships.* Networks integrate agents' complementarities in knowledge, capabilities and specialisation.
4 *Demand.* Demand can be both domestic and international.
5 *Institutions.* These include norms, routines, common habits, established practices, rules, laws, standards and so forth. Institutions may be formal (such as law and regulation) or informal (such as norms). Institutions significantly affect the rate of technological change, the organisation of innovative activity, and performance.
6 *Knowledge base.* Any sector has a specific knowledge base, technologies and inputs.
7 *Main processes and co-evolution.* Innovation is a process that involves systematic interactions among a wide variety of actors for the generation and exchange of knowledge relevant to innovation and its commercialisation (Malerba, 2002, pp. 250–251).

Using this concept, Part II will explore technological learning in strategic sectors, namely, electronics, automotive and food industries. National and sector actors and institutions can influence the technological capabilities development of firms.

Chapter 7: Thai electronic industry

The electronic industry is the largest industry in terms of its contribution to export. The industry is very much dominated by Western and Japanese TNCs. Most Thai firms are subcontractors producing parts and components. Compared to neighbouring countries like Malaysia and Singapore, TNCs in Thailand have less technologically sophisticated activities, for example, labour-intensive assembly. Local firms have been also technologically passive learners. The weakest areas are upstream activities, like IC design and wafer fabrication. Nonetheless, the hard disk drive (HDD) sub-sector performed much better than others due to the active roles of TNCs, better partnerships with local suppliers, and the availability of sector-specific public and private intermediaries and tax incentives.

Chapter 8: Thai automotive industry

Thailand's automotive industry started earlier than neighbouring countries, in the 1950s. Like the overall economy, it has experienced different policy regimes from import substitution to export promotion and liberalisation. Like the electronics industry, it has been dominated by TNCs, especially Japanese auto-makers. Thai suppliers were very concentrated in less technologically sophisticated parts. Nevertheless, unlike the electronics industry, Thailand moved up the global value chain. Several foreign automakers started to invest in more sophis-ticated activities, like design, advanced testing and engineering. Large Thai suppliers set up technology development centres. Industrial policy worked better in this industry, as government designated product champions of the one-ton pickup truck and eco-car. Thailand Automotive Institute was also an important intermediary in sector-specific promotion, linking TNCs with local firms, and firms with universities.

Chapter 9: Thai seafood industry

Unlike the electronic and automotive industries, the seafood industry has been dominated by large local firms. Some became TNCs investing in both developed and developing countries. Nonetheless, many local SMEs are still technologically weak. This chapter sheds the light on different strategies in technological development and innovation between these two groups of firms. Interestingly, product innovations in this industry illustrated the convergence of various disciplines in science, art and services, which are not commonly found in other manufacturing sectors. Roles of universities in human resource development and research, sector-specific government regulators and promoters, industrial associations and non-profit organisations are investigated.

Notes

1 By analyzing historical income transitions, the threshold number of years for a country to be in the middle-income trap is calculated. This cut-off is the *median number of years* that countries spend in the lower middle-income and in the upper middle-income groups. A threshold value of *14 years* to cross the upper middle-income to high income (US$5,000 to US$11,750) was calculated (Felipe et al., 2012).
2 According to the country's gross national income (GNI) per capita in 2012, countries have been classified as follows: low income, US$1,035 or less; lower middle income, US$1,036–US$4,085; upper middle income, US$4,086–US$12,615; and high income, $12,616 or more. As expected, the World Bank's measures and categories have been constantly adjusted since the official World Bank classification started in 1989.
3 Five cases include Chile, the Dominican Republic, Ireland, Jordan, and Singapore.

Part I
Thailand's national innovation system
Performance of key actors

2 Science, technology and innovation policy of the Thai government

This chapter explains the key characteristics of Thailand's science, technology and innovation (STI) policies, especially those concerning industrial upgrades. In the past 50 years, they were some changes in policies, but the primary goals have not changed much. These policies became long-lasting habits. Several have become the doctrine and mantra chanted by successive generations of policymakers. They were officially documented in successive five-year national economic and social development plans, a policy statement by the government that is delivered to the Parliament, and other national plans like industry master plans and science and technology plans. These policy habits differ from those in Asian countries that have successfully upgraded industries. We highlight these policies and compare them with those in more successful Asian economies.

2.1 Seven ineffective habits of Thailand's STI policy

Policy habit # 1: R&D promotion is the most important STI policy

Many policymakers equate the promotion of technology and innovation capabilities of the country with promotion of R&D investment. The ratio of gross expenditure on R&D (GERD) to GDP is one of the leading indicators used to formulate STI policy. For example, according to the National Science, Technology and Innovation Policy and Plan 2012–2021, the Thai government set a target of achieving 1 per cent and 2 per cent of GERD to GDP by the years 2016 and 2021, respectively.

Before the government of Prime Minister Thaksin Shinawatra (January 2001–September 2006), the scope of S&T policy in Thailand was rather narrow. It only covered four conventional functions, namely, R&D, human resource development, technology transfer, and S&T infrastructure development. This narrow scope of S&T was based on the so-called 'technology-push' R&D model or 'linear model of innovation', that is, the results of R&D should be readily designed and engineered to become new processes and/or products to be sold. This model was to be popular after WWII until the 1960s. Nonetheless, it has faded in other countries. Academics and policymakers in other countries realise that innovative processes are not automatic, and the failure rate can be high. It is also necessary to effectively manage the actors (government, private sector, funding institutes and market, and academia) participating in all relevant functions from R&D to design, engineering, testing and marketing and the back and forth interactions between these functions.

More importantly, for developing countries, R&D is usually not a *primary* source of innovation. This is because firms in these countries have evolved as 'learners', not radical innovators, by borrowing and improving technology already commercialised by innovating firms from developed countries (Amsden and Hikino, 1993). More successful latecomer firms in Korea and Taiwan, before producing more original innovations, have developed strong capabilities for generating 'continuous incremental change' in technologies initially acquired from forerunner countries. In less-successful latecomer firms elsewhere, including Thailand, the accumulation of this technological capability of firms has been much more limited (Bell and Pavitt, 1995). The World Bank's study on Thailand (see Arnold et al., 2000) stipulates that only a small minority of large subsidiaries of TNCs, large domestic firms and SMEs have R&D capabilities, while the majority are still struggling with increasing design and engineering capabilities. For many SMEs, the key issue is to build up more basic operational capabilities, together with craft and technician capabilities for efficient acquisition, assimilation and incremental upgrading of fairly standard technology. Therefore, the most important inputs for technological progress in a country like Thailand (more so than R&D) are technology absorption capacity, design activities, engineering developments, experimentation, training and the exploration of markets for new products. Government policies should enhance firms' capabilities in these areas. As late as 2015, the tax incentives provided by government agencies were beginning to cover non-R&D innovation activities. Tax incentives offered by the Department of Revenue increased from 200 to 300 per cent of actual R&D expenditures and expanded to cover firms' expenditures towards licensing foreign technology to advance their product and process innovations. The Board of Investment (BOI) introduced a new 'merit-based' investment promotion scheme in 2017 that also covered non-R&D technology upgrade activities like product design, packaging design, advanced technology training, licensing fees of intellectual property rights, collaboration with universities, and the development of local suppliers (Suchinai, 2017).

Policy habit # 2: firms are the 'users' of STI generated by universities and public research institutes

Firms must compete internationally, in contrast to universities and public research institutes. However, due to the influence of the linear model of innovation, the dominant orientation of policy and resource allocation for building technology development capabilities, since the 1960s, has focused on the capabilities and resources of scientific, technological, and training institutions that were intended to undertake technological activities 'on behalf of firms'. Conversely, policy measures and resource allocations designed to strengthen technological learning, technological capabilities, and innovative activities 'within firms' and knowledge flow among firms and between firms and other actors in innovation processes were rather minimal and ineffective (Arnold et al., 2000, p. ix).

Policy habit # 3: building indigenous technological and innovative capabilities is not a major economic policy objective

Unlike Japan, Korea and Taiwan, science and technology elements were not part of broader economic policies, namely, industrial policy, investment policy, trade policy and, to a lesser extent, education policies (see Intarakumnerd et al., 2002). The Ministry of Science and Technology was not considered an economic ministry until as late as 2016, and it has more roles in promoting technology development than economic agencies, such as the Ministry of Industry (Arnold et al., 2000, p. vii). This imbalance is very different from NIEs and Japan, where economic organisations like the Ministry of International Trade and Industry (MITI) of Japan (see Johnson, 1982), the Economic Development Board (EDB) of Singapore (see Wong, 1999), and the Economic Planning Board of Korea (see Chang, 1997) have significant roles in an array of policy and institutional support for industrial technology development.

Trade policy, where tariffs are the most important in Thailand, was not used strategically to promote technological learning, as in NIEs (see Amsden, 1989; Chang, 1994; Lall, 1996). Instead, trade policy was influenced by macroeconomic policy, for example, to reduce domestic demand for imports to balance payment deficits. The Ministry of Finance, the dominant agency which controlled the policy, had little knowledge or experience of industry and industrial restructuring (Lauridsen, 2002). Industrial policy in Thailand did not pay sufficient attention to the development of indigenous technological capabilities, which is an integral factor in industrialisation (Sripaipan et al., 1999, p. 37). In 2016, the Thailand 4.0 Plan was introduced. It aims to change the country into a value-based and innovation-driven economy by promoting technology, creativity and innovation in focused industries. Subsequently, the Law on National Competitive Enhancement for Targeted Industries was enacted. The Act seeks to promote investments in line with the Thailand 4.0 Plan. Incentives are given to promoted projects of the targeted industries. Remarkably, apart from tax incentives, the Fund for Enhancement of Competitiveness for Targeted Industries was established with US$ 285 million in government seed money for investment projects engaged in R&D or human resource development in specific areas.

Nonetheless, with the exception of the automotive industry, there were no reciprocal performance-based criteria (such as export, local value added, or technological upgrade targets) set for providing state incentives, like in Korea and Taiwan (Amsden, 1989, 2001; Amsden and Chu, 2003). Investment promotion privileges, for example, were given away once approved.

The National Research and Innovation Policy Council (NRIC), chaired by the prime minister, was set up in 2016, which aimed to integrate previously separated research policy with STI policy, to integrate science, technology and innovation issues with broader economic policies, and to enhance cross-ministry coordination. The members of this council are ministers from key economic ministries, in addition to the minister of science and technology. The secretariat of the council was jointly operated by the National Research Council of Thailand (NRCT) under the Prime Minister Office and the National Science, Technology and Innovation Policy Office under the Ministry of Science and Technology. It is too early to evaluate whether this council will achieve its objective. However, previous super-ministerial committees and councils failed to achieve their goals, since the prime minister did not actually chair the meeting, the meetings were infrequent and there was a lack of mechanisms to execute, monitor and evaluate resolutions approved by such committees.

Policy habit # 4: selective policies for particular sectors or clusters are market distortions

Economic policies were heavily influenced by the World Bank's 'market-friendly' approach to industrialisation, given the neoclassical economic inclinations of leading Thai technocrats; they were limited to so-called 'functional' interventions, such as promoting infrastructure building, general education, and exports, in general. There were virtually no selective policy measures, such as special credit allocations and special tariff protections, that targeted particular industries or clusters, as they were regarded as market distortion by mainstream economists. The exception was the automobile industry. Despite relatively liberal policy for the automotive industry, Thai government successively raised the local content requirements for automobile manufacturers investing in Thailand (see detailed discuss in Chapter 8).

A major change in policy came under the Thaksin government (2001–2006), when Thai government had serious "selective" policies addressing specific sectors and clusters for the first time. The government declared five strategic sectors which Thailand should pursue: automotive, food, tourism, fashion and software. Clear visions were given to these five sectors: 'Kitchen of the World' (food cluster), 'Detroit of Asia' (automotive cluster), 'Asia Tropical Fashion', 'World Graphic Design', and 'Animation Centre' (software cluster), and 'Asia Tourism Capital'. The cluster concept was introduced, which goes beyond the linear model of innovation by focusing on interactive and collective learning among firms and between firms and other actors in close geographical proximity. Thailand was divided into 19 geographical areas. Each area had to plan and implement its own cluster strategy that focused on a few strategic products or services. It was supervised by the so-called 'CEO Governors', who were given authority by the central government to act as provincial chief executive officers (CEOs). At the local level, the cluster concept was applied to increase the capacity of grass roots economy in the name of 'community-based clusters', especially to help the 'One Tambon One Product' succeed. Nonetheless, the actual implementation of the concept had mixed results because of misinterpretations of the concept of policy practitioners at the implementation level, policy discontinuity, inadequate trust and participation of concerned actors, and a lack of champions in the private sector in several cases (Intarakumnerd, 2006). Further, the Thaksin government did not consider long-term industrial upgrades beyond short-term and politically branded schemes. For example, it scraped the most ambitious upgrading plan, the Industrial Restructuring Project (IRP), which was initiated by an earlier government and went through an extensive consultation processes with the private sector. The IRP was going to upgrade 13 sectors with eight sets of measures, ranging from equipment modernisation to labour skills and product design (Doner, 2009).

Since 2015, BOI's 'Super Cluster' incentive scheme was introduced to upgrade the existing five industries and encourage the emergence of five new industries for the future development of Thailand. Two new cluster-like mega projects were implemented: the Eastern Economic Corridor (EEC) and Food Innopolis. The EEC consists of the three Eastern provinces, Rayong, Chonburi and Chachoengsao, with a combined area of 13,285 square kilometres. The EEC will see investments of US$ 43 billion during the next five years, mostly through foreign direct investments. The EEC is intended to accommodate investment in 10 targeted industries that are important for Thailand's future: next-generation cars, smart electronics, affluent medical and wellness tourism, agriculture and biotechnology, food, robotics for industry, logistics and aviation, biofuels and biochemicals , digital content, and medical services. Private enterprises investing in the EEC will receive a superb incentive promotion package which goes far beyond the current BOI's incentives, including preferable corporate and personal income tax privileges, longer terms of land leases for investors, a fast-tracked environmental impact assessment, and the direct use of foreign currencies in trade without exchange into Thai Baht.

Food Innopolis is located at the Thailand Science Park, under National Science and Technology Development Agency. This project seeks to position Thailand as a global food innovation hub in the global food industry. The expected availability of resources for the Food Innopolis include 3,000 researchers, 10,000 students in food science and technology, 9,000 food factories, 150 food research laboratories, 20 pilot plants and 70 universities. Food Innopolis belongs to one of the BOI's Super Clusters. Tax-based incentives include exemption from corporate income tax for up to 8 years, with an additional 50 per cent reduction for five years, and the exemption of import duty on machinery. Non-tax incentives include permission to own land and facilities while visiting on visas and work permits. However, whether these two initiatives will be successful or not depends on implementation, which is usually problematic in Thailand due to the lack of long-term commitment and coordination between concerned agencies.

Because of the general lack of and late introduction of selective policies, very few institutions have been founded to support the development of indigenous technological and innovative capabilities of firms in specific sectors. Most research institutes in the country fit the 'Jack of All Trades but Master of None' model. They have too many missions: assisting industry, building up S&T manpower, educating the general public about S&T, helping disadvantaged groups of society, and so on. They usually cover a broad range of technologies, with no specific targets for particular industries, and their linkages with the industry are rather weak. Further, sectoral promotion institutes under the Ministry of Industry, like the Thai Textile Institute, the Thailand Automotive Institute and the National Food Institute, are preoccupied with their own financial survival, since, due to short-sighted policy design, they must be financially independent after being a public organisation for five years. As a result, they rely on short-term moneymaking activities, like training to generate quick income, at the expense of activities promoting long-term development of firms in the sector. The situation in Thailand is quite different from countries like Taiwan and Korea, where there are many government research institutes with clear missions dedicated to strengthening the technological capabilities of firms in particular sectors and sub-sectors or even specific products.

Policy habit # 5: Transnational Corporations (TNCs) should be left alone

There is institutionalised belief among policymakers that the primary target of government policies should at Thai-owned firms, especially SMEs. Beyond providing tax incentives to attract foreign direct investment (FDI) to bring in foreign exchanges and generate employment, TNCs should be left alone. This is because they assume that TNCs a) will leave Thailand to invest in other countries; b) keep high value creation and value-added activities like R&D and product design at home; c) make all important decisions the headquarters of the TNCs, and policymakers in host countries have little influence on such decisions. These assumptions are not true these days. Unlike portfolio investment, FDI is much more difficult to move. Local conditions, such as the availability of knowledge workers and skilled labour, capabilities of local suppliers, size of the local market and sophistication of local demand, and working environment vary from country, and it is not easy to imitate. Moreover, the largest TNCs are engaging in more R&D and innovative activities outside their home countries. More interestingly, TNCs are now setting up R&D facilities outside developed countries that go beyond adaptation for local markets. R&D of TNCs affiliate is targeting global markets and integrated into core innovation efforts of TNCs (Patel and Pavitt, 2000). Between 1994 and 2002, the developing countries share of all overseas R&D by American TNCs increased from 7.5 per cent to 13 per cent. Foreign-owned R&D laboratories in China, for example, has reached 700 (UNCTAD, 2005).

More interestingly, several recent studies (Ariffin and Bell, 1997; Marin and Bell, 2006; and Hobday and Rush, 2007) point out that subsidiaries of TNCs in several countries, including the electronics industry in Thailand, have more autonomy in making decisions than conventional wisdom suggests. If correctly formulated and implemented, the policies of host countries can influence TNCs to invest in technologically sophisticated activities and generate spillover impacts to local economies. Like Thailand, Singapore is another country where FDI has been very much encouraged. However, it has specific government measures to generate spillover effects from FDI, in terms of development of local technological capabilities. Started as early as the 1970s, the Local Industry Upgrading Programme executed by Singapore's Economic Development Board (EDB), for instance, specifically aims to exploit knowledgeable and experienced engineers from TNCs to train employees of local firms to develop skills considered 'critical' for technologically upgrading high-priority industrial sectors (see detailed discussion in Chapter 5).

Unfortunately, partially due to conventional wisdom on the roles of TNCs, there was no such explicit and proactive link between promoting FDI and upgrading local technological capabilities in Thailand until as late as 2004, when the BOI launched the STI policy incentive for firms investing in R&D, employing university graduates in S&T, and training their personnel and those of their suppliers. Even so, the number of projects approved under the STI scheme has been relatively small, and the incentives to train suppliers' employees, the most deliberate attempt to generate spillover impacts from FDI, have been abolished (Chokdee Kaewsang, deputy director general, BOI, personal communication, July 10, 2007). Hopefully the new merit-based incentive scheme introduced by the BOI in 2017, as mentioned earlier, can bring closer knowledge-intensive collaborations between TNCs and local firms.

Policy habit # 6: government grants and direct subsidies to promote firms' technological learning should be constrained, if not prohibited

There are advantages and disadvantages inherent in different forms of incentives – tax concessions, loans and grants. Tax incentives are non-discriminatory; they are open to all firms that meet the stated criteria, and their administration is relatively simple. On the other hand, grants are generally more effective to promote focused activities prioritised by the government, and, unlike tax incentives, they are less likely to subsidise activity that would have occurred in any case (Turpin et al., 2002).

In Japan, the government tried to create "intellectual clusters", that is, regional clusters of universities, public R&D institutions, relevant institutes and knowledge-intensive core companies. The central government provided a five-year financial subsidy to cluster plans that were initiated by local governments, together with local universities and local firms, that passed a selection process. The aim was to foster interaction between the original technological seeds at public research organisations and universities and the business needs of regional companies to create a chain of technological innovations and new industries (see MEXT, 2002). In other Asian NIEs, like Taiwan, Singapore and Malaysia, grants were used effectively to promote specific activities (see detailed discussion in Chapter 5).

Alternatively, in Thailand, grant schemes to promote specific activities to enhance the technological learning of firms were rather limited. This is because, as mentioned earlier, fears of market distortion obstructed progress, and rigid government regulations emerged from fears of corruption and cronyism. There-fore, Thailand is missing opportunities to use effective and more-targeted policy tools, and it has to rely only on tax incentives, a blunter but easier to handle instrument. A detailed discussion of innovation financing schemes in Thailand will be provided in Chapter 5.

Policy habit # 7: increasing the number of graduates at the postgraduate level is the most critical S&T human resource development issue

Policymakers, especially those who came from scientific disciplines at universities, strongly believe that the most critical issue in S&T human resource development is to significantly increase the numbers of masters and PhD graduates. This might be true for teaching and basic research at universities and public research institutes, but several studies (TDRI, 2004; NESDB, 2007b) have confirmed that firms in Thailand, local and foreign, do not need extra graduates from the postgraduate level. Their primary concern, instead, is on the quantity of 'quali-fied' bachelor's degree and vocational certificate holders. Production-based firms and those conducting R&D primarily require only graduates with bachelor's degrees.

An interesting example is Toyota Motor, which recently started to carry out design and development work in Thailand by setting up the Technical Centre of Toyota Motor Asia Pacific Engineering & Manufacturing (TMAP-EM) in August 2003 at Samutprakarn Province. The centre focuses on material develop-ment, design and engineering to fit local needs and the testing of parts and vehicles. The primary difference from their production subsidiaries is that the centre employs more engineers than technicians. Notably, more than 90 per cent of engineers hold bachelor's degrees. Less than 10 per cent have master's degrees, and only two have PhDs. Executives of the centre view bachelor's degree holders as qualified to conduct development work at the centre, and there will be no need to increase the number of postgraduate engineers in the future. More interestingly, engineers, regardless of educational background, perform the same tasks and are trained in-house both locally and in Japan for one and one-half years. Despite satisfactory engineering knowledge, Thai engi-neers, in Toyota's opinion, lack language proficiency, creativity and group discus-sion ability, which are indispensable qualifications for research engineers (Omura, vice president, TMAP-EM, personal communication, April, 7th, 2008).

The overemphasis on postgraduate work comes at the expense of other skills. Policymakers have neglected an emphasis on vocation education. As an latecomer industrialising country, Thailand has a window of opportunity to exploit and upgrade technologies already developed by forerunner countries. Nonetheless, to seize such an opportunity, qualified engineers and technicians at the shop floor are very necessary inputs for firms' technological absorption capacity and 'incremental' innovation in a time of technological catch-up. Even though the Vocational Education Act and relevant laws exist, the lack of focus and the negative societal value on vocational education deters a sufficient accumulation of vocational students and technicians in the manufacturing sector. Vocational students and graduates are perceived as inferior human resources to students and graduates in general studies. This is very different from the situation in Japan, Taiwan and Korea, where the importance of vocational education has been highly regarded by the government and viewed positively by citizens, especially during their technological catch-up period, when innovations were mostly incremental and emerged from the shop floor. 'Project-execution' capabilities are important for latecomer firms to enter new industries (Amsden and Hikino, 1993).

2.2   Politics of STI policies

Why were the aforementioned seven habits so persistent in Thailand? One important answer lies on the perceptions of Thai policymakers. Two groups of Thai policymakers dominate STI policies and industrial development policies. One is the neoclassical economists-cum-bureaucrats, the so-called 'technocrats' in key economic ministries, who strongly opposed state intervention (especially selective and vertical industrial upgrade policies). The emergence and empowerment of technocrats were very much shaped by sociopolitical circumstances in Thailand. Technocrats gained authority in policymaking during many years of successive military and semi-democratic regimes. This process started with a military coup by Field Marshall Sarit Thanarat in 1957. Several macroeconomic agencies dominated by technocrats, mostly graduates from top universities' mainstream economic departments in the US and UK, were set up shortly afterwards, namely the Budget Bureau, Office of the Fiscal Policy, BOI, and National Economic and Social Development Board (Doner, 1992). Together with military generals, they dominated policymaking and implementation processes during the governments of Field Marshall Sarit and Field Marshal Tanom during 1958–1973. Later on, successively elected governments were too short-lived to initiate any long-lasting policies that differed from those of the technocrats. The military returned to power again in 1976, and the technocrats enjoyed further policy successes during General Prem's administration (1980–1988). The subsequent elected government were also short-lived, though the influence of the technocrats was reduced. The 1997 Constitution empowered elected governments and brought the Thaksin administration into power with an overwhelming majority in Parliament. As noted above, the Thaksin regime initiated several policies that were clearly different from those of technocrats. The two military coups in 2006 and 2014 were attempts of the establishment, including the technocrats, to regain authority in the policymaking process (see a more detailed discussion on the rise and fall of the Thai technocrats in Phongpaichit and Baker, 2014).

Another powerful group is the scientists-cum-policymakers, who were in charge of making science and technology policies. Many were well-known university professors and executives who later became administrators of national public research institutes and funding agencies. They had amicable relationships with the economic technocrats and also gained authority during military and semi-democratic regimes. They strongly believed in the linear model of innovation and paid significant attention to pro-science policies emphasising R&D and S&T human resource development. This was different from Japan and successful East Asian NIEs, like Korea and Taiwan, where the policymaking process was typically captured by engineering and economic development 'technocrats' who believed in the importance of industrial and technology upgrades 'within' firms (Amsden, 1989; Johnson, 1982; Lauridsen, L. 1999, 2008).

2.3   Conclusion

The competitiveness of a country is not a long-lasting phenomenon. It requires continuous upgrades and, sometimes, major transformation. Factors that used to underpin competitiveness in the past might transform into those reducing competitiveness in the future. Therefore, the ability of a country to learn to create new factors is very important in maintaining its global position. Successful late-industrialising countries evolved as learners. Thailand's learning abilities are doubtful. At the same time, new competitors like China, India and Vietnam and transitional economies of Eastern Europe are trying their best to enhance their learning abilities. Thailand needs to improve their learning abilities. Nonetheless, these seven policy habits are detrimental for Thailand's survival, let alone prosperity, in a learning economy. It is very important to break away for these habits and think alternatively, as suggested earlier. Changing of the mindset of policymakers is an essential prerequisite.

3 Technological learning and innovation of firms in Thailand

This chapter is about industry. We will examine previous studies on the technological capabilities and innovation of firms in Thailand. R&D and innovation surveys will be analysed to understand the type and degree of innovation in firms with different characteristics, especially in terms of size, ownership and specialised business sector. The sources of information and knowledge, barriers to innovation and collaborating partners in innovation will be investigated. In addition, we will illuminate the roles of private sector intermediaries in facilitating knowledge transfer and collective technological learning of firms.

3.1 Overview of firms' technological capabilities for development and innovation

Several studies of firms in Thailand conducted since the 1980s state that most firms have grown without long-term improvements in their technological capabilities, and their technological learning has been very slow and passive (see Bell and Scott-Kemmis, 1985; Chantramonklasri, 1985; Dahlman and Brimble, 1990; Tiralap, 1990; Mukdapitak, 1994; Lall, 1998). According to Arnold et al. (2000), only a small minority of large subsidiaries of TNCs, large domestic firms and SMEs have R&D capabilities, while the majority are still struggling with increasing their design and engineering capabilities. For a very large number of SMEs, the key issue is building up more basic operational capabilities, together with craft and technical capabilities for efficient acquisition, assimilation and incremental upgrades to fairly standard technology.

The slow technological capability development of Thai firms is quite different from Japan, Korea and Taiwan. Firms in these countries moved rather rapidly from mere imitators to innovators. As early as the 1960s, Japanese firms became more innovative, invested heavily in R&D and relied less on the importation of foreign technologies (Odagiri and Goto, 1993). In general, firms in Korea and Taiwan, where industrialisation (beginning with import substitution) started at about the same period as in Thailand and were more successful in increasing absorptive capacity (of foreign technology) and deepening indigenous technological capabilities in several industries (see for example, Amsden, 1989; Kim,

1993; Lall, 1996; Hobday, 1995; Kim, 1997). In the electronics industry, for instance, Korean and Taiwan firms were able to improve technologies by exploiting institutional mechanisms, like providing assembly services as original equipment manufacturers (Oems) and/or providing designs as own design manufacturers (ODMs) to TNCs. As a result, latecomer firms in those countries could acquire advanced technology and access demanding foreign markets (see Hobday, 1995).

Nonetheless, after the economic crisis in 1997, there were a few interesting positive changes in industrial sectors in Thailand:

1   Several large conglomerates such as the CP Group and Siam Cement Group increased their R&D activities. One large conglomerate alone invested 500 million Baht in R&D in 1999. The crisis made the executives of those companies think that long-term survival depended on deepening their technological and innovative capabilities. They could not simply relying on importing off the shelf technologies and the knowledge necessary for simple production, as before.
2   Several smaller companies recently increased their technological efforts by collaborating with university R&D groups to stay ahead in the market or to seize the most profitable market section.
3   To be part of global value chains, several subcontracting suppliers in the automobile and electronics industries were forced by their TNCs customers/ partners to strengthen their efforts to modify product design and improve efficiency.
4   There were new and emerging start-up firms (less than 50 employees) relying on their own design, engineering or development activities. These companies were managed by entrepreneurs that acquired a strong R&D background while studying or working abroad. Many of them are "fabless" companies (Intarakumnerd et al., 2002). Nonetheless, the pool of potential entrepreneurs is relatively small, as the rate of enterprise creation per population is relatively low, and scientists, engineers or managers prefer to work for public agencies or large businesses (OECD, 2011).

3.2   Analysis from R&D and innovation surveys

The low level of technological and innovative capabilities and passive learning of Thai firms can be illustrated by R&D and innovation community surveys. The surveys were carried out by the National Science and Technology Development Agency (NSTDA) and, later, the National Science, Technology and Innovation Policy Office. R&D surveys were carried out every year, but the innovation surveys were conducted in the years 2003, 2008, 2011 and 2014. The number of firms performing R&D and innovating in the manufacturing and service sectors were 27 per cent and 23 per cent, respectively, in the year 2014 (Table 3.1). This shows moderate improvement in the innovation performance

Table 3.1 Percentage of firms performing R&D and innovating in Thailand's innovation surveys

	2003	2008	2011	2014
firms performing R&D	6.0%	2.43%	7.96%	27%
innovating firms	5.8%	4.24%	20.73%[1]	23%

Source: Reports on R&D/innovation surveys 2003, 2008 by NSTDA; and R&D/innovation surveys 2011 and 2014 by National Science, Technology and Innovation Policy Office.

Table 3.2 Types of products by global value chain: 2011

Type of firm	Types of products (% of total revenue)				
	Manufacturing arms of parent companies	OEMs	Original design manufacturers (ODMs)	Original brand manufacturers (OBMs)	Others (traders, etc.)
Thai firms	9%	20%	16%	25%	30%
TNCs/ joint ventures	21%	28%	16%	17%	18%

Source: Thailand Innovation Survey 2011, National Science Technology and Innovation Policy Office

of firms in Thailand, which corresponds to positive changes after the financial crisis in 1997, as mentioned earlier.

Nevertheless, Thailand's performance is still relatively poor compared to more successful Asian countries. Comparison between innovation surveys conducted in Thailand and Korea in 2011–2012 illustrates the differences, in terms of innovative capabilities, of these two countries. Companies in Thailand lag far behind companies in Korea with respect to innovation. More than 40 per cent of firms in Korea carried out innovations, compared to about 20 per cent in Thailand. It is also striking that a much higher share of companies in Korea carry out product innovations. This could be an indication that companies in Thailand are at the stage where they would rather use their resources to improve the production process than the product itself, which could hint about a rather OEM-oriented economy. TNCs and joint ventures in Thailand operate at the low end of the global value chain. Most of their products (67 per cent) are manufactured according to design specifications of parent companies and design specifications provided by external buyers and traders. Similarly, the products of most Thai-owned firms (59 per cent) are manufactured at the low end of global value chain (see Table 3.2). Not many companies in Thailand innovate both products and processes, which is very common in Korea. This reflects the more advanced innovation behaviour of companies in Korea.

In terms of size, smaller firms tend to engage less in R&D and innovation activities than larger ones, and when they do so, their activities tend to be less sophisticated. Conducting quality control or testing activities is quite common in Thailand, as over two-thirds of the surveyed firms carried out these activities in 2011. Smaller firms were less receptive and had less capabilities in absorbing external knowledge and technology. In general, a small number of firms conducted sophisticated R&D activities. Only 10 per cent of SMEs performed in-house R&D, compared to more than 25 per cent of large firms.

In terms of R&D intensity, TNCs and Thai-owned firms are quite similar. They only spent about 0.1 per cent of total sales on R&D. This is relatively low, compared to firms in other Asian NIEs. The propensity of firms performing R&D varied across sectors. The leading sectors were science-based industries, like chemicals and electronics, and resource-based industries, like food and rubber. In-house R&D expenditure was largely devoted to the development of new or improved products (65 per cent) rather than processes (22 per cent). Almost one-fifth of manufacturing firms had innovation, compared to only 5 per cent of service firms.

The primary barriers to innovation were the lack of qualified personnel, the high cost of innovation, and limited access to information on technology and markets. The cost of innovation was a more important obstacle to innovation for smaller firms. Interestingly, the primary sources of information used for innovation were those entities interacting with firms on regular basis, namely, customers, parent firms, suppliers and the Internet. More sophisticated sources of information such as patent disclosures, public research institutions and universities or business service providers were much less important.

Regarding external collaboration, a horizontal relationship between firms in the same or related industries was viewed as rather unimportant by the surveyed firms. Cooperative consortiums among competing firms to research particular technology or products, as occur in Japan or Taiwan, are very rare in Thailand. Also, as the intra-firm technological capabilities themselves are weak, as already mentioned, and the innovation–centre interaction generated from such links is, therefore, limited. On the contrary, firms tend have more vertical collaboration with their customers and suppliers.

University–industry linkages (UILs) in Thailand are weak. Firms do not regard university and public research institutes as important sources of information and knowledge. They do not collaborate intensely with local universities or public research institutes. They also perceive that technical support from local universities and public research institutes is relatively weak. Thus, most UILs projects are limited to consulting and technical services. More advanced projects are occurring in some outstanding cases. However, there are interesting features when firms that perform R&D and innovating firms are analysed separately or when different industrial sectors are compared:

•   Firms performing R&D and innovating firms have stronger UILs than those firms not performing these activities. The former perceive universities and public research institutes as relatively more important sources of knowledge, and they view support from universities and public research institutes in a more positive light.

- Firms performing R&D and innovating firms in science-based industries requiring more sophisticated science and technology capabilities for R&D and innovation activities, such as petroleum/petrochemical, electrical machinery, telecommunication, computer and R&D services have more intense collaborations with local universities and public research institutes than those in resource-based and labour-intensive industries. However, the food processing industry, a resource-based sector, also uses universities quite intensely as a knowledge source and to improve production processes.
- Firms that cooperate with industry are mostly locally owned. Older companies are more likely to connect with universities than very young start-ups, which contradicts the university spin-off hypothesis that is valid for high-tech regions of industrialised countries. In Thailand, SMEs are only cooperating with universities in very limited cases, since most do not carry out any technology-intensive activities such as R&D, design and advanced engineering. Joint innovation activities are more likely to occur with larger local companies in traditional sectors. Within the public research sector, universities are more important knowledge sources than government research institutes.

3.3   Roles of private sector intermediaries

This section analyses the roles and capabilities of non-profit organisations like trade and industrial associations, professional associations, and private networking/ bridging institutes in supporting the development of technological capabilities and the innovation activities of firms. Concerning innovation support, there are only a small number of these organisations disseminating knowledge and promoting the innovation capability of firms.

This is quite different from Japanese industry associations which play significant roles in the diffusion of knowledge and new technologies among member firms. For example, industry associations played a major role in establishing and running cooperative research in the camera industry and automobile parts industry in the 1960s (see Goto, 1997). Although Taiwan's trade and industry associations tend to be sponsored by the government rather than a voluntary gathering of private enterprises (see East Asia Analytical Unit, 1995), some successfully help members enhance their capabilities. The largest and most influential manufacturers association is the Taiwan Electrical and Electric Manufactures Association (TEEMA). This association has actively assisted members in upgrading manufacturing technologies, expanding international marketing abilities and developing operation management. In addition, TEEMA also serves as a bridge for communication between the industry and government.

In Thailand, the Federation of Thai Industries (FTI) and the Thai Chamber of Commerce (TCC) are the most powerful private sector organisations. Their influence on the government's economic policies is strong. They can pressure government and induce policy changes. Most activities, however, aim to protect their short-term interests and gain leverage in negotiations with government (Laothamatas, 1992; Phongpaichit and Baker, 1997a, p. 150), such as export quotas, import levies and tax schemes. They are not very active in promoting the innovation capability of Thai firms. History matters as well. Their members come from commercial capital, rather than industrial capital (Samudavanija, 1990, p. 275). Therefore, they pay more attention to short-term commercial gains than long-term capability development.

FTI and TCC voiced their needs and concerns in the Joint Public–Private Consultative Committee (JPPCC), in an attempt to receive investment privileges and commercial advantages (Phongpaichit and Baker, 1997b). The role of this committee was very prominent in mid-1980s, when the idea of "Thailand Inc.", which the government aspired towards during that period, was popular. Since then, both the FTI and TCC have represented the interests of the private sector in several national committees. However, the importance of JPPCC later substantially declined.

The roles of business associations and JPPCC have experienced another turning point under the Thaksin government (2001–2006). The government thought that JPPCC was rather passive and, finally, it changed the style of operation from large sporadic assemblies to less formal meetings every Friday. This new form of informal meetings between the prime minister and private sector led to clearer national strategic goals with more up to date concepts, such as the introduction of supply chain management and industrial clustering. From 2015, the military government tried to broaden public–private partnerships to cover civic society under the name 'Pracharat'. The idea is to form networks of various businesses (large, medium, small, wholesale, and retail, and local enterprises and multinational corporations) to move the country ahead in four important issues, including innovation and productivity improvement. Members of these businesses would be invited to discuss in which specific areas they could cooperate with the government. It is too early to evaluate the success of this initiative.

Though FTI and TCC, in general, do not emphasise long-term issues of technological upgrades and innovation, there is a small range of activities which aim to encourage the diffusion of technological knowledge among members. Examples are management consulting services, the promotion of ISO certification and clean technology, and training programs in energy saving, sanitary standard, entrepreneurial management, design and technological skills upgrading. These activities are more active in the 'strategic' sectors designated by the government. Firms in these industries are more open to change. Some sectors within FTI are more enthusiastic to change than others, especially those with explicit concerns about the loss of national competitiveness compared to other latecomer countries.

With regard to trust building among members, which is a kind of social infrastructure of knowledge diffusion and innovation, the roles of FTI and TCC are not very impressive. They could create some trust among members by congregation, by exchanging ideas and opinions and sharing information among members. Trust primarily emerges gradually from joint activities such as marketing campaigns and trade fairs. However, internal organisations of the FTI and TCC are politically divided.

There are a few private sector organisations that specialise as bridging institutes that diffuse knowledge within the national innovation system. Technology Promotion Association (Thailand–Japan) or TPA is the most prominent. TPA's activities are in education, training and technical services. With a 40-year history, TPA has supported firms with various technical aspects, such as instrument calibration, productivity improvements, IT and automation and manufacturing management. TPA is also actively involved in the Thai government's policy of strengthening SME capabilities and entrepreneurship. In addition to general private sector intermediaries, there are also sector-specific intermediaries. The roles of these sector-specific intermediaries will be discussed in Chapter 7, Chapter 8 and Chapter 9.

3.4   Conclusion

To summarise, technological and innovative capabilities of firms in Thailand, both TNCs and Thai-owned firms, were relatively low, and technological learning was relatively slow in the past 50 years of Thailand's industrialisation. Nonetheless, after the financial crisis in 1997, there were some improvements, as TNCs and large local firms started to invest more in building sophisticated technological capabilities in product and process designs, advanced engineering, and R&D. This is demonstrated by an increase in the number of firms performing R&D and innovation in more recent innovation surveys. However, these improvements were lopsided. Most firms, especially SMEs, are still relatively weak. If the country would like to overcome the middle-income trap, it will need many more innovative firms to drive a knowledge-intensive and more competitive economy. Private sector intermediaries also need to be strengthened to enhance collaboration among firms and between firm and other actors in a national innovation system.

Note

1 Like previous surveys, the 2011 survey onwards also followed the definitions of the Oslo Manual. However, many more descriptions of different types of innovation were provided. Therefore surveyed firms could better recognize whether they had innovation. This may explain why the figures of innovating firms were higher than previous surveys.

4 Universities and public research institutes

Today, both universities and public research institutes are perceived as knowledge creating and intermediary agencies that can help firms enhance their technological learning. This chapter examines the roles in universities and public research institutes in supporting the technological learning of firms in Thailand.

4.1 Roles of universities in Thailand's national innovation system

The evolution of the Thai university system will be described. Subsequently, we will consider links between universities and industry.

4.1 Evolution of the Thai university system

Thailand's educational system grew significantly after World War II. Enrolment expanded from 15,000 students attending a total of five universities in 1961 to 100,000 students enrolled in 17 universities in 1972 (Anderson, 1977). Indeed, accelerated industrialisation in the 1970s led to a labour shortage in science and technology that, in turn, prompted the creation of open universities and distance learning institutes. Continued expansion resulted from the industrial boom from 1985–1995. The last quarter of the 20th century witnessed the growth of education's share in the national budget (from one-sixth to one-quarter), the opening of new private and public colleges, and a significant rise in the numbers of Thais obtaining education in the U.S. By 2006, Thailand had 20 public, four autonomous, and over 50 private universities (Schiller, 2006). The result was a 20-fold rise in the number of Thais with tertiary education (reaching 3.4 million) over this period (Phongpaichit and Baker, 2005). Graduates of the growing number of universities initially became officials; but as the expansion of bureaucratic positions slowed in the 1980s, most became professionals and managers in the private sector (Phongpaichit and Baker, 1995).

By the mid-1990s, the education system exhibited several important flaws. First, low-income and rural citizens have generally lacked access to higher education. Second, the focus of secondary curricula has tended to be on university preparation rather than on actual labour market requirements for vocational

Table 4.1 Number of graduates in the fields of science and technology

Academic year	Bachelor's degree	Master's degree	PhD
2009	96,173	8,172	608
2011	91,746	9,468	1,182
2014	86,231	4,755	580

Sources: Office of the Higher Education Commission and Office of the Education Council

training. Third, the research performance of Thai universities is substandard both in terms of industrial needs and sheer numbers. With regard to industry needs, Schiller (2006, p. 74) notes that research in Thai universities and research institutes "is done for the private sector, but not in interaction *with* it." In terms of numbers, one statistic – the number of publications listed in the Science Citation Index (SCI) – is disturbingly illustrative: in the 1980–1984 period, Thailand's SCI publication total of 394 exceeded those of Korea (341) and Singapore (253); by 1985–1989, the Thai figure had risen to only 446 compared to 1,043 for Korea and 597 for Singapore; by 2013, the Thai figure was 8,631 compared to 58,844 for Korea and 10,659 for Singapore. Finally, the numbers of Thai graduates with bachelor's, master's and PhD degrees in the fields of science and technology decreased during the period from 2009 to 2014 (see Table 4.1); the quality of these graduates, especially in math, science and engineering, also lags behind regional and world standards, resulting in far fewer engineers and scientists per capita than more advanced neighbours such as Singapore, Taiwan, and Korea (Ritchie, 2010).

Most universities in Thailand are primarily devoted to teaching. Only nine universities[1] were awarded 'research' university status and received an additional 3000 million Baht per year (US$100 million) to conduct research. On average, the contribution of university research to GERD was around 25 per cent in 2014, while the private sector and government agencies contributed around 54 and 20 per cent, respectively. Nonetheless, in terms of patents (key outputs of R&D), only 5 per cent of total patents were granted to universities during the same period. This signifies the universities' limited industrial relevance and ineffective R&D and Intellectual Property Rights (IPRs) management processes.

The levels and structures of funding in Thailand have contributed to weak performance in higher education. Schiller (2006) concludes that government funding for higher education had stagnated as a portion of GDP (around 0.5 per cent), as a portion of government expenditures (around 3.5–4 per cent), and as a portion of education spending overall (around 15–20 per cent). In addition, funding tends to be based on new study programs and research units, and on the bargaining power of each institution. Further, the accounting methods used by universities make monitoring difficult.

To address these problems, the government proposed several revisions, including more demand-based funding, a different budgeting system and more performance-based indicators, but the most important reform was support for university autonomy. The 1999 Education Reform Act mandated that all universities become autonomous within the next five years. Making universities autonomous from civil service had been part of the ongoing reform debate, as far back as the 1970s. Without autonomy, reformers argued, universities would lack incentives to demand high-quality research and teaching from faculty. Without a change in the incentives and focus of the faculty, universities were likely to remain disconnected from the needs of the private sector. More autonomy would provide universities with more flexibility and incentives to encourage professors to interact and collaborate with the private sector. At present, there are 24 autonomous universities in Thailand. KMUTT was the first to change its status to autonomous university in the early 1990s. Three universities were established as autonomous universities from the beginning: Suranaree University, Walailak University and Maefahluang University. The rest became autonomous later. It is worth noting that the transformation of several established universities to autonomous status happened with a military-backed government, following the coups in 2006 and 2014. This suggests that exceptional political autonomy is required to overcome resistance from faculty and administrations enjoying civil servant status in long-established universities.

More than ten years following passage of the educational reform act, observers would agree that reform in educational practice has lagged well behind political rhetoric. There is a widespread perception among the Thai public that the impact of these reforms has yet to reach schools and classrooms in significant ways, or on a substantial scale. Due to such failures, a second round of education reform was launched in 2009 with three primary objectives: significant improvement in education quality, increased access to education and participation from all sectors of the public. Nonetheless, there were not substantial changes and the next round of reform has been encouraged again and again.

A study by Liefner and Schiller (2008) shows real gains, in the case of KMUTT, after becoming autonomous. These include improved administration of human resources, budgeting, and academic affairs; greater latitude for initiative by the university president; and greater targeting of resources towards all functions, including industry outreach. Indeed, it seems that autonomous universities such as KMUTT, Suranaree, Khon Kaen and Mahidol have become more nimble, more tightly networked and more technologically savvy than the older, more established universities, like Chulalongkorn and Thammasat. As older civil service faculty retire, their positions are converted such that new faculty are only hired to replace them as members of an autonomous university, with expectations in line with the tenure system in the West. In the meantime, the development of links with industry has been slowed by gaps between older civil servants and newly hired faculty.

However, even the more autonomous and specialised science and technology (S&T) universities have yet to generate clear positive results. For example, Mahidol University (MU) was the first university to form a company, STANG Holdings, to invest in university spin-offs. Since 2004, only three technical service companies have been established by the firm. Most of those companies are still operated by university staff. Problems hindering commercialisation include the difficulty of selling and commercialising MU products due to general risk aversion towards business start-ups, a lack of marketing ability within MU, and the modest size of the firm's current venture capital fund (Virasa, 2008).

4.2   University–industry linkages

University–industry links (UILs), since the 1990s, have been promoted by the Thai government through the initiation of several policies. The National Science Technology and Innovation Policy and Plan 2012–2021 stipulates following measures:

- In the next five years, ten centres of excellences are to be established every year among universities, public research institutes and government agencies. These organisations can submit government proposals to set up centres. If selected, each centre will receive a government subsidy of 15 million Baht (US$ 300,000) each year for five years. The selection of specialised centre disciplines should be based on industry demand.
- Three regional science parks are to be established in major universities in the north (Chiang Mai University), northeast (Konkaen University), and south (Prince of Songkla University) of Thailand. In 2012, the cabinet has approved 8,634 million Baht for the development of these three science parks over three years (2013–2015). About 6,300 million Baht (US$ 210 million) is for infrastructure, and about 2.3 million Baht (US$ 77,000) is for operation costs, including all related activities (Akeanong Pleaksakul, Manager of Science Park Strategy and Collaboration Section, NSTDA, personal communication, March 13, 2013).
- Geographical area-based networks of industry, university, local government agencies and communities are to be strengthened to solve local problems and demand.

The Higher Education Development Project, financed in part by a loan of US$59.32 million from the Asian Development Bank during the period of 1999–2005, included additional reform to improve UILs. This reform created seven centres of excellence that were designed to foster collaboration between universities and the private sector. Despite some progress, most of these reforms have not met expectations or shown early signs of promise.

Moreover, the government has tried to strengthen UILs by encouraging universities to set up technology licensing offices and business incubators. The Office of Higher Education Commission provided funding to support incubation activities in universities in three phases: an idea-to-product phase, an incubation phase and an acceleration phase. So far, there have been 56 university business incubators grouped into nine geographical regional networks. There was also a failed attempt to introduce a law similar to the US's Bayh–Dole Act, which would enable universities to own intellectual property rights resulting from government-funded research.

In 2012, the Thailand Research Fund (TRF) initiated Research and Researchers for Industry Programme to provide research funding to students pursuing master's or doctoral degrees. The research topics are based on industrial demand. In 2014, the Thai government started operating Talent Mobility Programme, which intended to encourage university researchers to work in industry as full-time or part-time staff. Researchers who receive scholarships from the government are able to join this program. Time working in industry is considered compensation for these scholarships

Despite these efforts, UILs have remained relatively weak and fragmented. At the same time, other processes of innovation in Thailand have at least remained constant or, in some cases, improved. For example, a proportion of *design* patents granted to Thai nationals and firms compared to foreign ones has increased to 60 per cent of the total in latter half of 2000s, although foreign firms still own a majority of granted *invention* patents (see more discussion in Chapter 5). Brimble and Doner (2006) argue that this overall weakness is fostered by low levels of collective action among firms and a generally low level of interest in R&D. Thai universities often find a mismatch between their own R&D efforts and the interests of local firms, especially SMEs. The mismatch is exacerbated by different working cultures. Over time, a number of factors – weak academic capacity, mismatched supply and demand between universities, TNCs and leading local firms and a political system marked by fragmented bureaucracies – have undermined incentives for faculty collaboration with firms and diminished the credibility of universities as a viable innovation partner for firms (Schiller and Brimble, 2009).

There are, however, some bright spots. A few universities that were started or have moved out of the government bureaucratic structure have begun to successfully position themselves as value-added partners in several growing industries, including information technology electronics, agriculture (primarily rubber and energy crops), automotive, pharmaceuticals and nutraceuticals and medical products and devices. This suggests that, while generally weak, UILs were stronger in some sectors than in others.

4.2   Public research institutes

For public research institutes, there are ten organisations. Some of them, like National Science and Technology Development Agency (NSTDA) and the Thailand Institute of Scientific and Technological Research, carry out research in rather wide-ranging areas. Some are technology-specific research agencies, such as National Synchrotron Research Laboratory, National Astronomical Research Institute of Thailand, Office of Atoms for Peace and Geo-Informatics and Space Technology Development Agency. The rest, like National Institute of Metrology and the Department of Science Service, are responsible for setting metrological standards and providing technical testing services to private companies, respectively.

Here we will examine the roles of NSTDA, because it is Thailand's largest public research institute with a mission to support industries.

NSTDA, Thailand's leading autonomous funding and research organisation, was established in 1991. Three specialised centres – Genetic Engineering and Biotechnology (BIOTEC), Metal and Materials Technology and Electronics and Computer Technology (NECTEC) – were integrated under NSTDA umbrella. These three centres were established in the 1980s, in line with global trends at the time and the perceived local need for strong research capabilities in these areas. Nanotechnology Centre (NANOTEC) was created in 2003. In 2015, NSTDA had 2,700 employees (20 per cent of whom were PhD holders) and a budget of around US$200 million (NSTDA, 2015).

Roles and mental model

NSTDA takes a 'broad-based' systematic approach to enhancing the entire S&T system of Thailand to support national economic and social development. NSTDA's primary mission is to support R&D to strengthen Thailand's sustainable competitiveness, which is complemented by technology transfers and the development of human resources and infrastructure in S&T with outcomes that affect society and the economy. This mission indicates that the linear model of innovation is the key mental model of the organisation. In other words, NSTDA's primary mission is to undertake scientific research and then transfer the results to users (private firms and others). However, NSTDA also has a responsibility to build human resources and S&T infrastructure (laboratories, standards and testing and calibrating facilities). NSTDA's missions are very broad.

Since the mid-2000s, NSTDA has embraced the role of knowledge broker by facilitating knowledge transfer to local firms and enhancing their absorptive capacity. This was most explicitly demonstrated in the establishment of Technology Management Centre (TMC) in 2005. TMC has a mission to accelerate the development of knowledge-based industries in Thailand through a holistic and effective technology management system. This is primarily achieved by upgrading the technological capabilities of Thai SMEs by providing technical consultation, commercialising NSTDA's intellectual property and other selected technologies and funding financial assistance schemes. Following this, NSTDA seeks to grow knowledge-based companies and entrepreneurs through the provision of R&D facilities in science parks and its incubation facility.

However, NSTDA's new role as a knowledge broker requires different competencies. The ability to persuade and cooperate with other actors, especially private firms, is a strong requirement. The greatest challenge is how to connect the research side of the organisation, which has been locked into the organisational routine of building R&D capabilities since the very beginning, with the private sector support side (and existing knowledge-brokering activities). Most researchers in the laboratories, who comprise the majority of the workforce of NSTDA, have limited experience dealing with the private sector.

Degree of specialisation

Before 2006, NSTDA had no specific targets for either industrial sectors or geographical clusters. Research was instead based on the interests of researchers and their previous work (especially that conducted during overseas study). Due to recent changes in government policies and a more performance-oriented budgeting system, NSTDA was forced to work more extensively on the government's strategic sectors. The 6th NSTDA's Strategic Plan (2017–2021) focuses on supporting national targeted sectors, as mentioned in Chapter 2, namely, modern agriculture, future foods, biofuels and biochemistry, digital, modern automotive and transportation, electronics, robotics and automation, high-end services and tourism and health and wellness. Even with this adjustment, NSTDA's mission remains very broad, as it focuses on strengthening manufacturing and service industries and also on helping communities and needy people, which require very different capabilities and approaches. Closing down failed departments or projects is quite difficult. This has resulted in weaker management power to pursue core innovation capabilities.

Management

All NSTDA executives hold degrees in scientific disciplines, mostly from world-class educational institutes in developed countries. Many were formerly professors at public universities, and they have extensive research experience. However, most have not worked in the private sector or liaised closely with private firms. As a result, the dominant early vision and thinking paradigm and leadership of NSTDA was geared towards the creation of new knowledge through research. Although not an official policy, NSTDA strongly depends on R&D, with a more minor interest in supporting the development of technological capabilities within private firms. This secondary priority encompasses several financial and technical support schemes, such as technical consultant services, intellectual property services, training services and quality control services.

Strategic position in the government sector

NSTDA falls under the Ministry of Science and Technology, which was, until 2016, not considered as an 'economic' ministry. It was viewed as one of the least influential ministries, and few politicians wanted to be the minister in charge.

Technology transfer mechanisms

Technology transfer in NSTDA used to be through 'linear' mechanisms, such as licensing. However, more interactive modes of collaboration, namely, contracted and joint research ventures, have become more important. This reflects how NSTDA's research is now more oriented towards the needs of industry. In addition, NSTDA's science park, in the second phase of development, houses around 80 tenants. Most residents make up the R&D departments of large firms and are technical service providers, rather than start-ups under incubation. The number of successful graduated start-ups that have made initial public offerings is small. The second phase, in line with NSTDA's strategic plan, targeted large Thai and foreign firms in specific industries, namely, the food and automotive industries.

Revenue

Most of NSTDA's revenue comes from the annual government budget. Revenue from the private sector and competitive bidding on government projects is relatively small, although it has recently increased due to the aforementioned collaborative research projects. The share of total revenue generated from these sources was not set as a publicly announced target to be achieved within a certain period.

4.3 Conclusion

Thai universities and public research institutes, like NSTDA, have been under greater pressure to contribute to the development of firms' technological developments and innovations. There are positive signs of improvement in some universities and public research institutes, as they became more focused, in terms of research specialisation, and applied more interactive modes of collaboration, like contracted and joint R&D ventures with industry and incubation. Nevertheless, in spite of government policies encouraging closer links with industry, it is difficult for universities and public research institutes to change their own organisation routines, create new core competencies required for more interactive modes of collaboration or blend them with the existing research competencies.

Note

1 They are Chulalongkorn University, Thammasat Univerisity, Kasetsart University, King Mongkut's University of Technology Thonburi, Chiang Mai University, Prince of Songkla University, Mahidol University, Khon Kaen University and Suranaree University.

5 Innovation financing

This chapter will shed light on the effectiveness of innovation financing mechanisms in Thailand, compared with three Asian economies in Asia, namely, Taiwan, Singapore and Malaysia. These three economies seriously embarked on industrial development at more or less the same time as Thailand, in the 1960s. While Taiwan and Singapore have become high-income economies, Thailand and Malaysia are still upper middle-income economies. It will be interesting to examine if and how these financing mechanisms influenced the technological development of firms in these economies. This chapter draw extensively on 'Towards Effective Policies for Innovation Financing in Asia', a study under the author's leadership for the International Development Research Centre of Canada in 2010–2011 (Intarakumnerd and Wonglimpiyarat, 2012).

Four types of financing mechanisms will be examined in turn: tax incentives, grants, loans and equity participation.

5.1 Tax incentives

Singapore, Thailand, and Malaysia have R&D tax incentives based on R&D expenditure (double deduction), while Taiwan has adopted R&D tax credits. Since 2015, Thailand increased the R&D tax incentives to 300 per cent (triple deduction). Tax incentives based on R&D expenditure allow firms performing R&D to deduct expenses more than the cost of what firms have actually spent, while R&D tax credits allow firms to deduct a percentage of their R&D spending directly from companies' final tax liability. Singapore's tax incentive system has evolved according to the country's strategy and level of technological capability, unlike in Thailand, where the new BOI's merit-based schemes targeting knowledge-intensive activities was introduced as late as 2017.

When Singapore wanted to attract the labour-intensive electronic industry from the US and Japan, its government offered 'pioneer status', with attendant tax holidays of up to 15 years and other benefits, to TNCs to invest in *strategic* projects in Singapore. From the late 1980s to the late 1990s, when the strategy shifted to position Singapore as an R&D hub of TNCs, the government launched

Table 5.1 Comparison of tax incentives in Thailand, Malaysia, Singapore and Taiwan

Years of operation	*Thailand*	*Malaysia*	*Singapore*	*Taiwan*
	1996	*1982*	*1960s*	*1991*
Type	Tax incentives on expenditures	Tax incentives on expenditures	Tax incentives on expenditures	Tax credits
Coverage	R&D (strict definition), training, collaboration with universities; started to cover other innovation activities and became merit-based as late as 2015 and 2017, respectively	R&D, commercialisation of R&D	Pioneer activities, R&D, R&D hub (covering R&D outside Singapore), design, acquisition of intellectual property right and automation equipment	R&D, training, using certain technologies
Focus (sector, cluster, technology, type of firm)	General	General, specific (biotechnology, information and communications technology, East Coast development region), and firm-specific (pre-packaged incentives)	Pioneer status (strategic activities and sectors); convertible to grants for start-ups	General and specific (automation, energy saving, pollution control and digital technologies)
Project-by-project approval	Yes	No	No	No
Effectiveness	Number of approved projects increased but still from limited number of firms	Increase in number of projects but decline in number of firms applying	Increase in number of firms doing R&D in Singapore, especially transnational corporations	Number of approved tax deductions in Taiwan new dollar has increased, but no significant changes in number of applying firms; increase in employment, GDP and net tax revenues

Source: Intarakumnerd and Wonglimpiyarat (2012)

the Research and Development Tax Deductions Programme. Unlike in other countries, this deduction included R&D activities that took place outside Singapore (but were related to and benefited those in Singapore), although the deduction rate was lower than for those local activities. It seems that Singapore's government officials understand how global R&D networks of TNCs operate and what constitutes an R&D hub. Beginning in the late 1990s, when Singapore emphasised indigenous innovation by high-tech entrepreneurs, the government initiated the R&D Incentive for Start-Up Enterprises Programme. It was designed to meet the needs of R&D-intensive start-ups, which usually spend the first few years developing products and incurring losses. Tax exemption is therefore not useful to them. It also allowed these start-ups to convert an equivalent amount to what the companies would benefit from R&D tax credits if these companies profited to cash grants during the initial years. Since 2010, firms have been able to deduct 400 per cent of their expenditures from their income, subject to a cap of SGD800,000 from innovation activities, including R&D, design, registration and acquisition of intellectual property rights and the acquisition of automation equipment. The government realises that successful innovation needs more than R&D: it needs the support of a combination of several activities.

Taiwan's tax credit programme covers direct R&D activities and also expenditures on critical activities to upgrade firms' activities: automating production, reclaiming resources, controlling pollution, using clean and energy-saving technologies and using digital information technologies more efficiently. The experience of Taiwan illustrates that, like Singapore, it understands how to implement government incentives to tackle companies' technological upgrade problems.

Malaysia implemented a double deduction programme more than 10 years earlier than Thailand. Malaysia's R&D tax incentive schemes also have a much wider scope than Thailand's, dealing with R&D activities and also the commercialisation of R&D findings. As late as 2015, tax incentives in Thailand changed to cover other innovation activities. Apart from a double and later triple deduction of R&D expenditure, Thailand's BOI initiated a scheme in 2003 to promote 'Skill, Technology and Innovation' by offering one to three more years of tax exemptions for companies already receiving standard tax privileges, if they conducted in-house R&D, in-house training, and R&D collaboration with local universities. Malaysia's tax incentive system is more selective than Thailand's. It has tax incentives for targeted industries such as information and communications technology (ICT) and biotechnology, activities such as medical device testing, and geographical clusters such as the East Coast Economic Development Region. Customised incentives based on the merit of each case – the 'pre-packaged incentives' – have also been introduced recently. The Super Cluster tax incentives targeting specific industries, geographical clusters and special economic zones (EEC and Food Innopolis) was introduced in Thailand in 2015 and 2017 (see Chapter 2). Therefore, Singapore, Taiwan and Malaysia had both generic and selective tax incentives much earlier.

Regarding the efficiency of tax incentives, only Thailand scrutinises companies applying for R&D tax incentives on a project-by-project basis, though after 2015, approved firms with reliable track records have been exempted. Other countries periodically conduct ex post evaluations of the overall impacts of tax incentives on firms' innovation and impacts on the economy. The Thai case makes the application process cumbersome and goes against the initial virtue tax incentive, which is supposed to be fast and almost automatic in application. The level of trust in Thailand's society is low, and the government has been worried about false claims. Thus, the Department of Revenues (responsible for the double deduction of R&D expenses) authorises the National Science and Development Agency (the largest public research institute) to verify whether submitted applications are R&D projects and whether their proposed expenses are appropriate. Since many proposals are submitted, the average approval period is as long as five to six months. Similarly, project-by-project approval is required for firms wanting to take advantage of the BOI's 'Skill, Technology and Innovation' programme and the new merit-based schemes started in 2017. The number of approved projects, however, has increased over the years. Likewise, in Taiwan, after 2000, the number of approved values, in terms of Taiwan dollars, has increased year by year, but the number of companies applying for such incentives has not significantly changed. Large firms in Malaysia and Thailand mainly benefit from R&D tax incentives but not SMEs, which do not have capabilities to conduct R&D.

Only Taiwan has conducted a formal study on the impacts of tax incentives. It found that tax credits for encouraging R&D, training, and automation have induced further R&D investment, leading to more jobs and higher GDP. As a result, there have been significant positive net effects on tax revenue (Liu and Wen, 2012). In Thailand, however, although one cannot observe direct causation, the results from community innovation surveys illustrate that innovative firms used R&D tax incentives more than non-innovative firms (see a comparison of tax schemes Table 5.1).

5.2 Grants

In Singapore, grants are the key instruments for financing the development of technologies and innovation. Singapore also has a greater variety of grant schemes that target all activities in value chains and evolve according to the country's level of development and the technological capabilities and needs of firms. In the 1970s and 1980s, Singapore initiated schemes such as the Local Industry Upgrading Programme to promote technological diffusion from TNCs to local enterprises. Under this scheme, the EDB subsidised a percentage of the salary of a manager sent by a TNC to work in a local enterprise for two years. As of 2010, more than 200 TNCs and 1,000 local suppliers had been involved in the programme. This is an illustration of systemic policies to leverage TNCs strength to upgrade local SMEs. Without these targeted policies, the spillover impacts from TNCs would be limited. Grant schemes were also given to individuals and companies to promote critical skills, such as ICT. In the 1990s, when firms in the country needed to increase their R&D capabilities, the government initiated a grant scheme to leverage Israel's R&D capability by funding feasible and collaborative R&D projects between firms in the two countries. Since the late 1990s, whenever the government has wanted to promote high-tech entrepreneurship and basic R&D, it has initiated grant schemes. For example, the Technology Innovation Programme covers 50–70 per cent of equipment, materials, labour, software and IPR costs of projects operated by individual SMEs and consortiums. The Innovation Voucher Scheme provides SMEs with grants to pay for consultants and technical services provided by reputable local and overseas universities and research institutes. The government also uses this scheme to promote intra-firm collaboration by allowing up to 10 SMEs to pool their vouchers. Singapore astutely uses government schemes to tackle systemic failures of its national innovation systems, that is, linkages among local SMEs and between local SMEs and public research institutes and universities.

The Technology Enterprise Commercialisation Scheme, based on open call and selection, is a competitive grant scheme that was launched in 2008 to support locally owned technology-oriented start-ups and SMEs at the proof of concept stage (to conceptualise ideas) and the proof of value stage (to carry out further R&D and develop a prototype). Specific grant schemes commercialise technologies developed by universities, encourage polytechnic institutes to conduct translational research on R&D outputs from universities and research institutes and bridge the gap between university and firm needs by allowing collaborating firms to license university technology once proven, without obligation if the project fails. Some grant schemes are aimed at strategic service sectors (e.g., aviation and animation) and strategic and future-oriented technologies and capabilities (e.g., logistics capability, environmental technology capability, medical technology capability, marine capability and tourism technology). These schemes are under the management of responsible sector-specific development agencies. Some grant schemes have been provided by universities to their students to start their own businesses. These government schemes targeting early-stage companies, however, have had only moderate success. For example, only one-fifth of surveyed firms were aware of the Innovation Voucher Scheme. Start-ups that have taken part in the recent schemes gave an average rating of 3 on the 5-point Likert scale on three criteria: meeting firms' immediate objectives, improving their long-term growth prospects, and helping them move to the next growth stage. The bureaucracy involved in the application processes must be lessened and awareness of the various schemes raised.

For many years and in various programmes, Taiwan has used grants as financial instruments to encourage firms to enhance their technological and innovative capabilities. As in Singapore, programmes in Taiwan have co-evolved with the development of firms' capabilities. Several programmes are sector or even product-specific. For example, when Taiwan firms gained production capabilities as subcontractors of TNCs and wanted to move up the global value chain by attaining product development capabilities, Leading Product Development was implemented in 1991 to subsidise R&D costs for high-tech products and expertise, such as those produced by the ICT, aerospace, pharmaceutical and semiconductor industries. About 800 of 1,600 cases were approved, almost evenly divided between SMEs and large firms. The results of the Leading Product Development were impressive, as TWD1 of grant induced about TWD10 investment in R&D, TWD21 investment in production and TWD42 in sales. On average, one project generated 3.7 patents and 2.9 derivative products (Liu and Wen, 2012). Similarly, when the government wanted to promote local start-ups, it adopted, as a model in 1998, the US Small Business Innovation Research Programme, which provided grants to firms in three phases: feasibility studies, R&D, and commercialisation. A more generic grant scheme, the Industrial Technology Development Programme, was initiated in 1999 to fund the preliminary study and R&D phases of firms attempting to develop forward-looking industrial technologies. TWD1 of grant induced TWD2.46 of R&D and TWD4.89 of capital investment (Liu and Wen, 2012). In the 2000s, grants were given specifically to strategic technologies and industries, such as conventional technology development, commercialisation of biotechnology and the knowledge-based service industry.

Similarly, Malaysia's Ministry of Science, Technology and Innovation has been providing various types of grants that cover the whole spectrum, from basic and applied research and prototype development (Science Fund) to the development of technology for commercialisation (TechnoFund) and innovation (InnoFund). The TechnoFund supports the development of a pilot plant, scaling up laboratory prototypes and field trials and testing. It also has provisions for the acquisition of IPRs from local and overseas entities to be further developed locally during the pre-commercialisation stage. The InnoFund has two categories of grants. The first assists individuals and sole-proprietors, microenterprises, and small enterprises in developing new products or improving existing products, processes, or services with elements of innovation for commercialisation (Enterprise Innovation Fund). The second grant type is used to assist community groups in converting knowledge and ideas into products, processes, and services that improve the groups' quality of life (Community Innovation Fund). This support for innovation at the bottom of the pyramid. In addition, the Cradle Fund provides support at the pre-R&D phase.

On another front, the MITI also provides several matching grant schemes to SMEs for business start-ups, product and process improvement, productivity and quality improvement and the enhancement of *targeted* capabilities in design, labelling, product packaging, and market development and brand promotion (including activities abroad). In addition to these general grant schemes, some schemes promote *strategic* technologies, industry clusters and products. The Multimedia Super Corridor R&D Grant Scheme was set up to assist local companies and joint ventures in developing multimedia technologies and applications to contribute to the overall development of the Multimedia Super Corridor. The Biotechnology R&D Grant Scheme was established in 2001 under the National Biotechnology Directorate to support biotechnology R&D activities and the commercialisation of research findings in specific areas of national importance to the biotechnology industry. Matching grants for developing halal products are also available. All these schemes are attempts to promote techno-logical and innovative capabilities in the private sector and to forge relationships between industry, universities and public research organisations. Most funds are devoted to applied and problem-solving research projects under the Tech-noFund. Although the administration of these schemes has not been formally assessed, it is problematic because project approval takes a long time (Thi-ruchelvam et al., 2012).

In administering grant programmes, Thailand is an exception. Grant schemes are limited in variety and size. The country relies more on indirect support to private firms through tax incentives and similar mechanisms. Giving *public money* to private firms gives rise to allegations of cronyism and corruption. Neoclassical economists, who dominate national economic policy agencies (and academia), do not like the idea of selective government interventions in particular industrial sectors, activities, clusters and firms, as these appear to be working against the market mechanism. The prospect of losing public money, if grant projects fail, is not acceptable to government authorities, especially those in charge of the budget. As a result, grants are mostly given to public research institutes and universities. Since 2008, R&D grants, such as those awarded by NSTDA to private firms, have been significantly reduced, even practically stopped. The most successful grant sources has been the Industrial Technology Assistant Program, started in 1992, which provides up to 50 per cent financial support for hiring consultants (freelancers or university professors) to help solve the technological problems of SMEs. More than 1,000 firms have received financial support from this programme. The results, however, have been mixed, as some firms did not carry out developmental activities by themselves after the projects ended. The factors correlated with success seem to have been active involvement of executives of firms, clarity of project goals, finding the 'right' and devoted experts, and, importantly, NSTDA's industrial technology assistants, who act as intermediaries between firms and experts.

Thailand's National Innovation Agency (NIA) also offers a grant scheme to support up to 75 per cent of expenses for prototyping and pilot scale activities of firms. It gives smaller grants than agencies in other countries (about US$160,000 for three years) and gave grants to only 56 projects during 2003–2007. Nevertheless, the number of supported projects significantly increased to 552 during 2010–2014. Recently, NIA has focused more on the strategic sectors of biotechnology businesses, design and solutions and energy and environment. In 2011, NIA adopted the idea of an 'innovation coupon': it gives grants to private firms equal to 90 per cent of the project cost to hire listed innovation service providers either for feasibility studies or pilot project implementation. FTI, the largest association of manufacturers, is a partner in the scheme to help NIA select the right projects. The results have yet to be seen. This is also true for the Fund for Enhancement of Competitiveness for Targeted Industries established in 2016, as mentioned in Chapter 2 (see a comparison of grant schemes in Table 5.2).

Table 5.2 Comparison of grant schemes in Thailand, Malaysia, Singapore and Taiwan

Year of operation	Thailand	Malaysia	Singapore	Taiwan
	1990s	2000s (becoming more unified)	1970s	1980s
Level of significance compared with other mechanisms	Not significant	Very significant	Very significant	Very significant
Coverage	R&D, prototyping and pilot scale	Whole spectrum: pre-R&D, R&D, R&D commercialisation, acquisition of other firms' intellectual property rights	Wide-ranging and evolving according to the needs and capabilities of firms	Wide-ranging and evolving according to the needs and capabilities of firms
Focus (sector, cluster, technology, type of firm)	General; became more sector-specific as late as 2016	Both general and specific (technologies, sectors, clusters and products)	Both general and specific (sectors, technologies and types of firms)	Both general and specific (sectors, technologies and products)
Effectiveness	Too small to have critical success	Criticism of lengthy approval processes and duplication of schemes	Effective older policies, e.g., Local Industry Upgrading Program, enhancing linkages between TNCs and local firms, but only moderate success with recent policy on promoting high-tech start-ups	Inducing substantial R&D investment from recipient firms, supporting creation of new industries or products. Small and medium-sized enterprises benefited significantly

Source: Intarakumnerd and Wonglimpiyarat (2012)

5.3 Loans

Loans are a more prominent innovation financing mechanism in countries such as Thailand. The NSTDA's Company Directed Technology Development Programme has been providing soft loans of up to 75 per cent of total project cost and less than US$1 million per project for R&D, product and process upgrading and building or refurbishing laboratories. The number of approved projects each year has been small (fewer than 20); recently it has become even smaller as selection criteria have become more stringent: the activities of firms must be related to R&D and employ technologies that are new to the industry. For example, the acquisition of machinery not related to R&D is unlikely to receive a loan. Most SMEs, therefore, are not qualified, since they do not have R&D capabilities, and the problems they face are more production related. Although NIA provides zero-interest loans of up to THB5 million for innovative projects for the first three years, setting up the scheme is problematic, as loans have to be channelled through commercial banks, whose usual selection requirements do not favour financially risky innovation projects. As a result, only 38 projects were approved during 2003–2007, which increased to 61 during 2010–2014.

In Singapore, loan programmes are much less prominent government financing mechanisms than grants and equity. As early as 1976, when Singapore was still trying to exploit technologies generated elsewhere, SPRING's Local Enterprise Finance Scheme was initiated to provide low-interest loans to automate and upgrade factories and equipment and to purchase factories. More recently, a programme was set up to help SMEs acquire working capital and machinery. A loan insurance scheme to help SMEs secure loans by providing insurance against default has become available, as well.

Taiwan has several loan schemes, including those for purchasing automating machinery for manufacturing and agriculture enterprises, revitalising traditional industries, purchasing energy-saving equipment, promoting industrial R&D and purchasing computer hardware and software. Firms in service industries, such as Internet and technical service providers, are also eligible. The loan per company is US$2–US$3 million. From the beginning of the schemes in the 1980s to April 2010, more than 50,000 cases have been approved. Both loans and approved projects are on a much greater scale than in Thailand. The SME Credit Guarantee Fund is also available to help SMEs secure loans from these government programs.

Malaysia has used loans as financial instruments since the 1970s and implemented many schemes for different purposes. Specific low-interest loan schemes for high-tech enterprises and entrepreneurs have been used to stimulate technology development and innovation. Loans for particular groups such as university graduates are also available. Schemes for strategic sectors (e.g., automotive, food), technology (e.g., adoption of automation technology, ICT), and activities (e.g., international branding) are also in place, as are more generic schemes. Credit Bureau Malaysia (formerly known as SME Credit Bureau) was incorporated in 2008 to give independent credit ratings to SMEs, which usually lack 'reputational collateral' for access to financing. The ratings are based on information from the Central Bank and financial institutions. The bureau is popular and trusted, with a membership of 27,000 SMEs and 38 financial institutions. Of course, the credit bureau does not directly evaluate firms' innovation performance, but they use indicators like previous business performance, include new businesses, new products and activities (see a comparison of loan schemes Table 5.3).

Table 5.3 Comparison of loan schemes in Thailand, Malaysia, Singapore and Taiwan

Year of operation	*Thailand* 1990s	*Malaysia* 1970s	*Singapore* 1970s	*Taiwan* 1980s
Level of significance compared with other mechanisms	Significant	Significant	Not significant	Significant
Coverage	Increasingly focused on R&D	Whole spectrum	Evolving according to needs and capabilities of firms	Wide-ranging and evolving according to needs and capabilities of firms
Focus (sector, cluster, technology, type of firm)	General	General and specific technologies, sectors and activities	General and specific activities	General and specific sectors, technologies and activities
Facilities supporting access to loans	SME credit guarantee	SME credit guarantee; SME credit rating agency	SME credit guarantee	SME credit guarantee
Effectiveness	Number of applications in some programs has dropped significantly	Applications increased significantly, especially from SMEs, but 90% of recipient firms are Bumiputra (Malay and indigenous ethics)	Not significant	Number of approved projects increased

Source: Intarakumnerd and Wonglimpiyarat (2012)

5.4 Equity financing

In Thailand, the venture capital (VC) industry was first established by foreign VC funds in 1987. VC investments generally target growth and expansion in the venture life cycle. The major organisations providing VC funds to support entrepreneurial development are Office of Small and Medium Enterprises Promotion, NIA, One Asset Management, Stang Holding and the Market for Alternative Investment (MAI) Matching Fund. The MAI Matching Fund, a fund of funds with assets of THB2,000 million, was set up to increase the number of newly listed companies (including VC-backed companies) on MAI. However, the fund ceased operation in 2010 because the track record was not successful. The Revenue Department also provides taxation schemes to support VC fund investments. These schemes assist VC funds and investors through corporate and personal tax exemption policies. VC funding in Thailand per company is THB720 million, on average, and they last about 10 years before exiting. Most VC funds invest 30 per cent in the early stage and 70 per cent in the growth and mature stages. The leading business angel in Thailand is the Thai-Chinese Business Association. Currently, the size of business angel investing is about THB90 million. The deal ranges from THB4 million to THB50 million, with no exit strategies (Scheela and Jittrapanun, 2010). This means that angel investors in Thailand do not really behave like those in more successful countries like US, who take a high risk and exit their invested companies when they become successful. Therefore, in practice in Thailand, innovative business at early and risky stages cannot be financed by the so-called angel investors.

In Malaysia, the VC industry began in the early 1980s with the establishment of Malaysian Ventures, whose primary aim was to invest in high-tech industries. The Malaysia Venture Capital Association was established in 1995 to develop a VC industry to further support technological innovations. The government is a major source of VC financing: most VC funds are channelled to Bumiputra (Malay and native ethnics)-owned and government-linked firms. The major organisations providing VC investment funds to support entrepreneurial activities are the Malaysia Technology Development Corporation, established in 1992 to provide financial support for multinational subsidiaries, and the Malaysia Venture Capital Management Fund, established in 2001 to support entrepreneurial activities of local high-tech firms. Only seven per cent of total VC funds in 2004, however, were invested in the start-up phase.

In Singapore, the government launches innovation financing schemes and programmes to support innovative firms, as most VC funds are set up with government co-funding (such as Temasek Holdings and Technopreneurship Investment Fund Ventures, which act as funds of funds), and they are managed directly by government agencies or government-linked companies (e.g., EDB Investments, Vertex Management, EDB Life Science Investment). These government VC funds invest in various sectors, mainly in government strategic areas of ICT, and subsequently, biomedical sciences, clean technology and digital media. To fill the gap of early-stage funding left by private VCs, a government VC firm called TDF Management was formed in early 1995. It provides seed funding to entrepreneurs and high-tech start-ups. Apart from funding through VC, the government provides 'direct' financing, especially to new entrepreneurs and start-ups. For example, the EDB launched the Start-up Enterprise Development Scheme, a co-financing scheme to take dollar-for-dollar equity stakes in promising start-ups backed by third-party private sector investors to fill a market gap in seed-stage funding (Mani, 2004). In 2008, the Early-Stage Venture Funding Scheme was founded to match SGD1 investments in early-stage technology start-ups with another SGD1 invested by selected VC firms. Singapore has also tried to groom its angel investment network, as business angel investors often provide seed funding to support the early stages of new venture development. Business Angel Funds, managed by SPRING, co-funds pre-approved business angel groups. Business Angel Funds and the Start-up Enterprise Development Scheme complement each other. A start-up that has already received funding from the Start-up Enterprise Development Scheme can still apply under Business Angels Funds for a follow-up investment of up to SGD1.5 million. This is an example of how well financing innovation schemes in Singapore are coordinated, which is not usually the case in other countries. Schemes to promote start-ups by particular groups of people, such as entrepreneurs under 26 years old, have also been made available. The effectiveness of these schemes is moderate. Results of surveys from about 300 start-ups revealed that about one-fifth of start-ups have participated in such government assistance schemes, with those in the very early stages of growth (i.e., pre-revenue firms) having a higher propensity to participate than those in later-growth stages. Still, since 2006, close to 5,000 new high-tech enterprises have been registered each year, and the growth rate of firms of high-tech enterprises has increased in recent years, partly because of government financing policy measures.

In Taiwan, VC financing began as early as 1983 with the implementation of the Regulation Governing Venture Capital Business Management to stimulate the development of the VC industry. VC investing is mostly done in the established, mass production and expansion stages, where the government plays a major role. The Taiwan Private Equity and Venture Capital Association was established in 1999 to encourage economic development. The Ministry of Economic Affairs supervises the management of VC funds. The success of VC development in Taiwan can be tied to the social and economic bridge linking its high-tech industry with the US's Silicon Valley. In addition to VC enterprises, Taiwan, like Singapore, also has government *direct* financing schemes. As early as 1973, the Development Fund was set up to directly invest in innovative companies and indirectly invest through VC firms. Strategic sectors such as biotechnology, aerospace and optoelectronics were the priorities. To stimulate the technological development of SMEs, the SME Development Fund was established in 1994 to invest directly and indirectly with government and private VCs. These two large funds are the government's primary investment arms to promote innovative firms and stimulate the growth of the VC industry.

The governments of Thailand, Malaysia, Singapore and Taiwan play a major role in promoting innovation with VC financing schemes that support companies with high growth potential (public sector interventions). Although the VC mechanism aims to provide risk capital to firms operating in high-risk environments, VC financing programmes are not effective in the early stages of entrepreneurial development. VC investment in these four countries tends to be available at the less risky, later stages (expansion), reflecting the funding institutions' aversion to risk. The angel investment network is not fully developed, except in Singapore, where it is a significant source of capital during the early stages of high-tech development. To overcome difficulties in early-stage financing, the governments in Singapore and Taiwan have initiated 'direct' equity financing programmes.

Only a small number of VC funds operate in Thailand, despite government policy that promotes the VC industry. In 2010, only two VC funds applied for a VC license. The total funds raised by Thailand's VC industry represent

0.15 per cent of GDP. In 2016, the Ministry of Science and Technology tried to launch a 500 million Baht (US$14.2 million) fund of funds for Thai start-ups in ten targeted industries under the umbrella of 'Startup Thailand', as mentioned in Chapter 2; however, it has yet to materialise. Providing funds to the private sector, even through VCs, let alone direct financing, is very problematic in Thailand.

In Malaysia, although the government is the main investor developing technology-based start-ups, the VC market's growth is slow because of the lack of human capital and the risk-averse behaviour of local VC firms. In Singapore, local high-tech companies have effectively used a variety of assistance schemes, such as Growing Enterprises Through Technology Upgrade, EDB, SPRING Singapore, International Enterprise Singapore and Political Risk Insurance Scheme. The effectiveness of these programs targeting start-ups, however, seems to be moderate. The number of firms is not large, but it has increased over the years. More importantly, the programs helped create awareness among Singaporeans, especially the young, about starting their own businesses instead of working for the government and TNCs, as before (Wong and Singh, 2012). In Taiwan, new VC investments have grown as a result of the government tax credit policies that support VC companies (new investments grew from 1,155 cases to 1,850 cases between 1998 and 2000) when the tax credit was available. The number of investments, however, decreased after the tax credits stopped (see Table 5.4 for a comparative summary).

Table 5.4 Comparison of equity financing schemes in Thailand, Malaysia, Singapore and Taiwan

Year of equity financing operation	*Thailand* 1987	*Malaysia* 1984	*Singapore* 1983	*Taiwan* 1983
Stages of VC investment	Expansion and mezzanine	Growth and expansion	Early, growth, and expansion	Established, mass production and expansion
Specialised funds to support innovative firms through VCs	SME VC Fund, MAI Matching Fund, Start-up Fund	MTDC, MAVCAP	TRIDENT Platform	Development fund and SME Development Fund
Sector of VC investment	Food and drink, machinery and equipment, household furnishings, wood products and costumes	Manufacturing, ICT and biotechnology	ICT, biotechnology, medicine, genetic engineering, software and technology-enabled business services	Optoelectronics, biotechnology and electronics

Year of equity financing operation	*Thailand* 1987	*Malaysia* 1984	*Singapore* 1983	*Taiwan* 1983
Formal venture capital association (VCA)	Thai VCA established in 1994	MVCA established in 1995	SVCA established in 1992	Taiwan VCA established in 1999
Business angel financing	Infancy stage of business angel clubs and networks	Infancy stage of business angel clubs and networks	Has formal business angel network (SPRING)	Has formal business angel network (TWBAN)
Government's direct equity financing	None	Several schemes targeting university graduate and young entrepreneurs	Several schemes by both government alone and co-investment with private VC	Large government funds (development fund and SME Development Fund)
Effectiveness	Low uptake in government VCs; private VCs are risk-averse; fund of funds initiative failed because of insufficient demand; lack of mentoring services	Helped sustain private sector R&D but not yet effective in creating new start-ups	Surveys show moderate success of new programs but the overall number of high-tech start-ups increased significantly, especially in the past few years	Helped increase high-tech start-ups but not significantly, as only 28% of VC funds went to early stages

Source: Intarakumnerd and Wonglimpiyarat (2012)

5.5   Conclusion and lessons learnt

The general differences between Thailand's innovation financing mechanisms and those of the other three countries can be observed as follows:

1   While financing schemes in the other three countries did change significantly in response to changes in innovation systems and the development level of the country, this has not been the case for Thailand. The country has generally been unable to change its schemes in a timely fashion.

2   Initiation of new types of schemes in Thailand came much later than other countries.

3   Most policy instruments in Thailand are, to a large extent, limited to tax incentives, mainly for R&D activities. In other countries, grants and public equity financing have been used extensively to finance activities ranging

from starting new companies, implementing new production technologies, engineering, design, R&D, R&D commercialisation, marketing and branding.

4   There is much less flexibility to remove ineffective instruments and/or convert instruments, such as converting a scheme from tax incentives to grants.

5   Only a few schemes 'selectively' target strategic sectors, clusters, activities or the developmental stages of firms.

6   Most incentives are offered and operated by Ministry of Science and Technology, not 'economic' ministries, as in the other countries. This confirms that, until recently, economic ministries had limited interests in technological upgrading, as described in Chapter 2.

7   Policy processes in Thailand are much weaker in terms of cross-agency coordination, monitoring, evaluation and learning.

6 Institutions

Institutions play a major role affecting the rate of technological change, the organisation of innovative activity, and performance. These include norms, routines, common habits, established practices, rules, laws, standards and so forth. Institutions may be formal (such as law and regulation) or informal (such as norms). This chapter will examine the impacts of three important institutions on the development of Thailand's national innovation system: entrepreneurship and trust, government's perception of its role in supporting the technological learning of private enterprises, and intellectual property right regime.

6.1 Entrepreneurship and trust

With the exception of Indonesia, the Thai economy is rather unique in Southeast Asia, because no class of indigenous 'big business' entrepreneurs exits. Even smaller businesses in Bangkok, especially retail, are mostly owned and operated by Sino-Thais (East Asia Analytical Unit, 1995, p. 78). The dominance of family-owned enterprises established by immigrant Chinese entrepreneurs in Thailand has long been rooted into Thai business norms and cultures. Therefore, historically and culturally, entrepreneurship in Thailand is not much different from Chinese-dominated countries like Taiwan.

In terms of trust, Chinese-owned businesses tend to be built as family-affiliated corporations that are managed based on ownership and kinship rather than skills. This "family-ownership-control-type business" (Suehiro, 1992, p. 392), characterised by low stock ownership diffusion and more familial CEOs has led to business and joint investment cooperation among different companies within the same family affiliates, *but only little* cooperation among various enterprises of different families (Suehiro, 1992, p. 390 and East Asia Analytical Unit, 1995, p. 78). Although many Chinese-run firms have grown into big conglomerates covering many business areas, the founding family still keeps the ultimate control. Then, firms under the same family umbrella overlap and compete, leading to intra-family conflicts. In sum, cooperation is less likely in inter-family businesses, and in intra-family enterprises, cooperation often causes family complexity and contention.

An effect of Chinese–Thai entrepreneurship on the failure acceptance attitude can be translated into two contrasting views. While the first view sees Sino-Thai influence as a threat towards innovation, owing to the low acceptance of failure and a lack of merit-based management, the second view sees the Chinese–Thai business culture as a positive condition that tolerates risky ventures that are needed for long-term planning and investment.

Firstly, because Chinese-run enterprises expand their businesses for the main purpose of their "total fortune of the family" (Suehiro, 1992, p. 403), they advance into areas such as finance and real estates. This evidence shows their risk-averse characteristics in doing businesses. The upfront profit from trading and property business is far more attractive than the expensive technology-intensive manufacturing that will only earn long-term gains. As a result, technological deepening or long-term sustainability is not a cause for concern. Political capability, in terms of gaining access to lucrative oligopolistic sectors, seems more important than technological capability in this case.

The structural and political context also affects the behaviour of Sino-Thai firms. Most of the domestic expansion and diversification rationale comes because Sino-Thai firms take advantage of government's industrial promotion and other tax incentives, while diversifying into foreign ventures for scale and scope purposes, given the limited domestic market and intensive local competition (Suehiro, 1992). Therefore, liberalisation and the high industrial growth of the 1980s, together with many outside favourable conditions unrelated to the fundamental capability of the Thai industries, drew Thai conglomerates into new diversification of technologies that were unrelated to their original businesses. The underlying capability these firms accumulated enabled them to establish and maintain political connections with government authorities, rather than their technological and innovation capabilities (see Intarakumnerd et al., 2002).

The second view, however, sees the Chinese–Thai entrepreneurship positively. The fact that "Sino-Thai families traditionally were reluctant to relinquish ownership and management of their companies . . ." (East Asia Analytical Unit, 1995, p. 80) allow them to create a long-term vision for their very own family businesses. While some list their assets in the stock market, many still prefer to raise capital conservatively, through loans and offshore bond issued with a chance to benefit from different international interest rates. The continuous vision from parents to children protects them from the short-term concerns of stock prices or threats of acquisition. Deep-rooted corporate culture and tacit learning by family members creates a qualified decision base for risky projects (Intarakumnerd, 2000, p. 16). Therefore, they are capable of pursuing risky ventures with the expectation of future success without being distracted by their stockholders.

Entrepreneurship in Thailand experiences interesting changes. The attitudes and behavioural changes towards entrepreneurship in Thailand come from exposure to modernism, innovative culture and new technologies of the West, which have infiltrated through overseas education among the predecessors of the new generation. This factor is where the two contrasting views of Sino-Thai business culture finally merge. The combination of fast decision traits and long-term plans will create a condition that enables Thai businesses to grow both horizontally and vertically. It will likely create a business structure, despite remaining as family-run, that becomes increasingly innovative and adaptive to the changing environment. The attitude that favours kinship rather than managerial skills has also started to change. Professionalism of management grows despite the tight family control (see Intarakumnerd, 2000), allowing better prospects for competency building and technology development.

The above description is likely true for large and established enterprises. Knowledge-intensive start-ups (newly emerged and fast-growing ventures aiming to meet marketplace needs by developing or offering innovative products, processes or services) may have different stories. According to GEM, Bangkok University and BUSEM (2012), Thailand has a high rate of entrepreneurial activity. However, while there is plenty of 'necessity-based' entrepreneurship (i.e., people who become entrepreneurs because they need to economically survive), such as in the case of street vendors, it is doubtful whether there is a critical mass of 'opportunity-based' entrepreneurs who seize and execute risky opportunities through innovations. Opportunity-based entrepreneurship is usually an important characteristic of successful start-ups. Innovation surveys show that risk-taking attitudes are rather low among Thai entrepreneurs, though it has improved in recent surveys. Thai traditional wisdom focuses more on conforming to existing societal values and the ideas of senior persons rather than challenging them.

6.2 Perception on the roles of government in strengthening private firms

Direct grants and public equity participation are quite limited in Thailand, both in terms of variety and the amount of support (see Chapter 5). This is because there is a long-standing subscription to neoclassical economic thinking among Thai bureaucrats. The market mechanism is believed to be the best way to allocate resources. Thus, government intervention should be limited. Firms should be able to help themselves. Government roles should be limited to providing adequate infrastructure and a favourable business environment, with transparent and stable rules. Selective innovation financing policies aiming to help particular sectors, clusters, types of firms or activities are viewed as market distortions. That is why there are a few grant and public equity participation schemes in general and even fewer selective ones (see Chapter 5). On the other hand, S&T policymaking has largely been in the hands of scientists who believe in a 'linear model of innovation'. Therefore, most schemes focus on R&D and neglect other aspects of capabilities development, including production, engineering, design, problem-solving, utilising other firms' knowledge and IPRs, branding and so on. Since innovation is narrowly viewed as commercialisation of R&D, other types of innovation, which are not led by R&D, like new services, new business models, new applications and solutions are very much ignored.

Corruption is a major concern in Thailand. There are concerns that grants and, to a lesser extent, direct equity participation from government will favour particular firms and individuals. This is one of the major reasons why direct support is lacking and why R&D tax incentives require project-by-project scrutiny. Similarly, 'selective' policies targeting particular industrial sectors, types of companies, products and activities are also subjected to this negative view.

There is a widely accepted notion of how 'public money' should be used. Public money must be recoverable. It should not be spent in the ways leading to no returns, despite good intentions. Government officials who authorise such spending are personally accountable, if mistakes happen. Therefore, grants, or even direct equity participation from government to finance the risky activities of firms or particularly risky types of firms, such as start-ups, are quite rare in Thailand.

6.3   Intellectual Property Rights (IPRs) regime

Patents have the greatest impact on industrial product and process innovation compared to other types of IPRs, like trademarks and copyrights. We will examine the evolution of the patent regime and its impacts on technological learning and innovation of firms in Thailand.

Evolution of Thailand's patent regime

Prior to the promotion of patent law in 1979, there had been no protection for human invention or design in Thailand, unless it could fall under other areas of intellectual property. Later, the Patent Act of 1979 was proposed to promote the R&D of new inventions and designs that are useful to domestic agriculture, industry and commerce and to offer legal protection to inventors and designers by prohibiting others from copying or imitating their intellectual innovations (DIP, 2006).

To protect Thailand's exports, particularly from countries which could pursue trade sanctions on Thailand because of the allegedly inadequate protection of intellectual property rights (especially the US Omnibus Trade and Competitiveness Act 1988: Section 301), the first amendment to the patent law was completed in 1992. The first amendment signified a change from weak to strong protection. The major changes included expanding the scope of patentable matters to food, beverages, pharmaceutical products and pharmaceutical ingredients, and extending the term of patent rights protection from 15 to 20 years after the filing date (see Kuanpoth, 2006). The amendment has also increased the rights of the holder of a process patent by including a monopoly right to import products produced directly by means of the patented process.

The second amendment was completed in 1999 to make the law comply with the Trade-Related Aspects of IPRs (TRIPS) agreement and other well accepted international standards. Under this amendment, the group of persons who may obtain patents in Thailand was extended to nationals, residents and those having a legitimate ongoing business address in any country that is a member of the Paris Convention or the World Trade Organisation (WTO). The one-year period from the first application for a patent for the invention anywhere in the world within which patent applications must be filed in Thailand was extended to 18 months. The number of exceptions to patent rights was reduced. The scope of compulsory licensing was restricted. Finally, a system of petty patents or the utility model was introduced. For a petty patent, an invention is eligible and accepted for registration if it makes the examiner believes that it is new and industrially applicable. Unlike patents, applicants of petty patents do not have to illustrate distinctive inventive steps. The initial term of a petty patent is six years from the date of filing with the possibility of two extensions of two years each. Petty patent is more suitable for incremental innovation which gives countries a greater chance to achieve during the catch-up stage. It is noteworthy that petty patents were introduced very late in Thailand to encourage local people to invent more and take advantage of this patent protection. This situation is different from that of the NIEs of East Asia, which introduced petty patents much earlier. These countries' first introduction of patent laws sought to promote local innovation (UNIDO, 2006).

In comparison with Japanese patent law, especially during the catch-up period of the 1960s–1970s, Thai IPR law seems to follow Japan's model by facilitating greater intra-industry technological knowledge flows and spillovers (Intarakumnerd et al., 2002). Firstly, foreign patents are not automatically protected under the current system. Foreigners wishing to protect their assets need to apply for a Thai patent no later than 12 months after filing abroad. Secondly, the system requires that all patent applications be disclosed 18 months after the applications are filed. Thirdly, applications for patents in Thailand tend to be applied for earlier in the innovation process because of a first-to-file rule of priority, in contrast to the first-to-invent rule of priority of the US. Lastly, Thai patents have a three month period of 'pre-grant opposition' when competitors or anyone else can challenge the validity of the prospective patent. In terms of licensing, patent licenses must be in writing and submitted to the Patent Office at the Department of Intellectual Property (DIP). It is not permissible to restrict the license to Thailand. A licensor may not require a licensee to pay a royalty for use of the patented invention after the patent term has expired.

To summarise, Thailand's patent regime has been changed from weak to strong. Since the late 1990s, the regime moved towards more protection, due to the TRIPS agreement, political pressure from advanced countries, and bilateral free trade agreements. This change has been successfully implemented because Thai policymakers believed that stronger patent regimes generally stimulate technological innovation and progress more. This belief is contradicted in empirical studies (such as Levin et al., 1987 and Cohen et al., 2002), which conclude that innovation would continue to appear in the absence of patent protection, that patents in general were not sufficient to appropriate all benefits from innovation, and that there are nation- and sector-specific differences in the use of patents for appropriate returns for innovation.

As Thai patent laws evolved, so did the governmental bodies implementing them. In 1992, the DIP was established to hold direct authority over registration, protection and efforts to increase public understanding of IPRs. In terms of patent registration, Thailand lacks qualified patent examiners. For instance, only 29 patent examiners evaluated 6,261 patent applications in 2006. Consequently, there has been a decline in patents granted in 2005–2006 (Posaganondh and Adsawintarangkun, Personal Communication, July 7th, 2007). Thailand joined the WTO on January 1, 1995, and the Intellectual Property and International Trade Court was established in 1996. This court is equipped with well-trained career judges and associate judges that specialise in the relevant fields so that it can effectively manage cases which are different from conventional disputes.

Regarding the knowledge diffusion aspect, Thailand lacked purposeful organisation, which encourages knowledge diffusion, and, hence, the learning of local firms (Intarakumnerd et al., 2002). Previously, the diffusion of information in patents was implemented in a 'passive' manner, as the DIP just sent information (without systemic digestion and classification to match different demands of each industrial sector) to business associations and provincial authorities under the Ministry of Commerce. The Intellectual Property Centre (IPC), which later undertook responsibility to diffuse the knowledge embedded in IPRs, was only just established in 2006. This centre is still a part of the bureaucratic DIP, whose main functions are the promotion of IPRs registration and protection (not diffusion of knowledge). This is different from the cases in Japan and Korea. In Japan, the National Centre for Industrial Property Information and Training (NCIPI) was set up as a part of Japan Patent Office to provide training services and promote the diffusion of information and knowledge embedded in IPRs. Similarly, the Korea Institute of Patent Information (KIPI), a non-profit organisation, was set up in 1995 to support the Korean Intellectual Property Office by providing patent information services to the private sector. KIPI has 350 patent analysts conducting patent research, patent analysis and patent evaluation. In Thailand, the situation is very different. The Thai IPC has limited resources and capacity to perform knowledge diffusion tasks. Importantly, it has no capability to analyse Thai and foreign patents, both in effect and outdated, to inform local firms of future technological and business opportunities which might arrive from those patents. Another organisation of IPRs-embedded knowledge diffusion is the 'Toryod' website (www.toryod.com) created by the unit for the creation of awareness and exploitation of patent documents for R&D, under sponsorship of the Thailand Research Fund (TRF) since 1995. The website provides links to a searchable patent database of several countries, including patent databases in Thai. However, this project has been operated with limited capacity.

The evolution of patent laws and relevant organisations is illustrated in Table 6.1.

Table 6.1 Evolution of Thai patent laws and organisations

	Patent Act 1979	1st Amendment (1992)	2nd Amendment (1999)
Reasons	To promote the R&D of new inventions and designs that are useful to domestic agriculture, industry and commerce To offer legal protection to inventors and designers by prohibiting others from copying or imitating their intellectual innovation	To avoid trade sanctions under s.301 To meet international standards, the drafters consulted a number of relevant sources, e.g., the Paris Convention for the Protection of Industrial Property, the Patent Cooperation Treaty, the World Intellectual Property Organisation (WIPO) Model Law, the draft Patent Law Harmonisation Treaty and the preliminary Draft Agreement on TRIPs	To make Thai patent law officially comply with the TRIPs agreement
Major changes	There was no law in Thailand that protected such creation and, therefore, the rights the plaintiffs were not recognised by the Thai legal system	Limitation of non-patentable subject matters Long-term protection and expanded scope of protection Establishment of a drug price review committee Modification of the process for the grant of compulsory licenses	National treatment Priority filings Patent rights (adopted the principle of international exhaustion of patent rights) Petty patents Compulsory licensing Drug Patents Board
Organisation	Department of Commercial Registration	DIP (1992) IP&IT (1996)	IPC (2003)

Source: Author

Impacts of the changes in patent regime

Compliance with TRIPS and general public acceptance of the importance of R&D, innovation and IPRs, has led to *atmospheric* changes, especially for government policy initiatives. The BOI, for instance, has launched a special investment package promoting 'Skill, Technology and Innovation'. Firms can enjoy one or two years of extra tax incentives if they perform the following activities in the first three years: spending on R&D or designing at least 1–2 per cent of their sales, employing scientists or engineers with at least a bachelor's degree as at least 5 per cent of their workforce, investing in training for their employees with least 1 per cent of their total payroll, and spending at least 1 per cent of total payroll on training personnel of their local suppliers. In addition, the National Science, Technology and Innovation Act, considered the 'basic law' on science, technology and innovation, was enacted in 2008 to provide a framework for public and private sector institutions to strengthen the nation's STI capabilities, which include S&T manpower, S&T infrastructure, public awareness of S&T, and S&T management and administration systems. Creating and commercialising IPRs is also emphasised by this new law. Compliance with this law requires management mechanisms for implementation, monitoring and evaluation systems and the flexibility of rolling improvement. According to the law, a new super-ministerial structure – the National Science, Technology and Innovation Policy Committee – was founded and will be chaired by the prime minister. Members of the Policy Committee include ministers from key ministries relevant to science, technology and innovation, together with respected resource persons. After the Abhisit Government came to power in 2009, government policies to promote a 'creative economy' based on creativity, talent and the unique culture of Thai people (the so-called Thainess) was initiated. Policymakers pay a lot of attention to 'creative industries' like Thai food, Thai crafts, Thai massage and spa, Thai films, Thai multimedia software and so on. Again, the issue of intellectual property right creation, protection and utilisation is an indispensable part of this new policy.

In term of *actual* impacts on patent registration, under the weak protection regime, patent registration was low and increased very slowly. In the period of 1979–1992, there were only 955 invention patents granted. Foreign firms generated almost 90 per cent. Even after the 1992 introduction of a stronger protection regime, which should have provided more incentives for patent registration, the use of patents to protect local invention and design is still low in Thailand. Just more than half of granted patents were for industrial designs, some of which involved rather low technological content. The foreign share of granted patents was still very high, at more than 90 per cent (see Table 6.2).

It is worth mentioning that under the 2nd Amendment of the Thai Patent Act (1999), the right to apply for patent protection was no longer restricted to Thai nationals and the nationals of countries with reciprocal patent agreements with Thailand. The right to apply for patent protection was extended to nationals of countries which were part of international patent treaties or conventions that Thailand was also a participant. Since Thailand is a member of the WTO, and thus TRIPS, nationals of other WTO member countries have received the same protection at the same level as Thai nationals. Consequently, there was a remarkable increase of invention patents after 1999.

Although the share of patents issued to Thai residents has increased gradually from 17 per cent during the weak patent regime of 1993–1999 to around 37 per cent during strongest patent regime of 2000–2016 after the second

Table 6.2 Granted patent by ownership and type of patent (1979–2016)

Year	Granted patents			Design patents			Invention patents		
	Total	Thai	Foreign	Total	Thai	Foreign	Total	Thai	Foreign
1979–1992 Weak patent regime	3,095 (100%)	742 (24%)	2,353 (76%)	2,140 (100%)	645 (30%)	1,495 (70%)	955 (100%)	97 (10.2%)	858 (89.8%)
1993–1999 Stronger patent regime	6,204 (100%)	1,081 (17%)	5,123 (83%)	2,296 (100%)	938 (41%)	1,358 (59%)	3,908 (100%)	143 (3.7%)	3,765 (96.3%)
2000–2016 Strongest patent regime	44,091 (100%)	16,460 (37%)	27,685 (63%)	27,316 (100%)	15,361 (62%)	11,955 (48%)	16,755 (100%)	1,045 (6.2%)	15,370 (93.8%)
Total	53,390 (100%)	18,229 (35%)	35,161 (65%)	31,752 (100%)	16,944 (54%)	14,808 (46%)	21,638 (100%)	1,285 (6%)	20,353 (94%)

Source: DIP

amendment of the patent law (see Table 6.2), the yearly number of patents issued to local inventors does not demonstrate any sign of significant increase, especially for invention patents which required stronger technological capabilities than design patents. The high degree of foreign dominance implies that local inventors have low technological capabilities to develop inventions that meet the basic requirements of novelty, inventive steps and industrial application.

In addition to private firms, the local S&T community is a very minor beneficiary of this particular incentive system. There was not a tradition or practice of using patent information in the basic or advanced education and research arenas such as universities and research institutes, or even in industry itself. It is only in the past decade that major Thai conglomerates like the CP Group and Siam Cement Group have seriously and actively promoted innovation and the use of the patent system to increase productivity and competitiveness (Intarakumnerd and Charoenporn, 2010).

As mentioned earlier, under the current generally stronger regime, petty patent or utility model system to promote knowledge diffusion and local innovation was introduced, albeit late. During 1999–2016, the number of petty patents annually granted grew dramatically from seven to 1288. The share of Thai owners granted petty patents, in total, increased from 72 per cent to 93 per cent during that period. This supports the idea that, at present, there are many local people and firms who cannot fulfil the requirements of the standard patent but can satisfy the requirements of a petty patent.

To conclude, the Thai IPRs regime, in general, has played a small role in the process of technological catch-up. In addition to the late introduction of petty patent, Thailand's IPRs system provided opportunities for technological diffusion from advanced countries and 'learning by imitating' during the period of the weak regime; most firms, however, failed to move from 'duplicative imitation' to 'creative imitation' and innovation. This is quite different from the experiences of Japan and East Asian NIEs. At one point, the Thai IPRs regime was a 'weak protection' without being 'pro-diffusion'. In effect, it was not really a 'catch-up mode' of IPRs regime. The difference from East Asia NIEs can be explained by the lack of 'preconditions' for technological catch-up. Beyond laws and regulation, these include the accumulated sufficient indigenous absorptive capacity of firms in the country, the mechanisms of knowledge diffusion and utilisation, and an innovative enabling environment (Intarakumnerd and Charoenporn, 2010).

6.4 Conclusion

The effects three important institutions have on the Thai national innovation system have been examined. On entrepreneurship and trust, the overseas Chinese type of entrepreneurship has both positive and negative effects on technological learning and the innovation of firms. It is quite obvious that the country needs to develop more opportunity-based entrepreneurs who can recognise opportunities, leverage external resources and take risks to start new businesses. Changes in the mindsets of policymakers about private sectors, corruption and the use of public money are required to support such new businesses. Regarding the intellectual property right regime, Thailand has lost an opportunity to develop a regime focusing on diffusion and exploitation of external knowledge when weak protection of IPRs was possible. Given the stronger protection of IPRs these days, the technological catch-up process is more difficult.

Part II

Sectoral innovation systems of strategic industries

7 Thai electronic industry

7.1 Overview of Thailand's electronic industry

Thailand joined the global value chain of electronic industry in the 1970s, at the same time as Malaysia and a decade after Singapore (Hobday and Rush, 2007). Between the 1970s and 1980s, Thailand became another assembly hub in Southeast Asia for diodes and capacitors (Chairatana, 1997), which was concentrated on downstream labour-intensive assembling and packaging activities. After the financial crisis, exports of electrical and electronic products increased sharply from US$23 billion in 2000 to US$45 billion in 2014. Most international trade in this sector is in intermediate goods, that is, electrical and electronic parts and components. The electronic industry workforce has increased from around 300,000 in 2001 to 400,000 in 2011, with an observable representation of migrant workers from neighbouring countries (Intarakumnerd et al., 2016).

At present, there are 2,034 firms in Thai electronic industry. The majority of firms are small and medium-sized enterprises (1,354 and 387, respectively) with a substantial representation of TNCs in both assembly and part supplying domains (EEI, 2012). TNCs (293 firms) dominate assembly activity with an extensive control over supply chain of parts and components (see Table 7.1). Central and Eastern regions of Thailand are among the most favourable locations for the industry, following by the Northeastern and Northern regions.

TNCs subsidiaries in Thailand have achieved substantial technical acquisitions and upgrades in the last two decades, while R&D activities for new products and process innovation are still mainly conducted outside the country (Hobday and Rush 2007). Research and innovation activities among Thai-owned large corporations are not as high, but they have also increased, particularly for IC and appliance designs. Most SMEs in the electronics industry are OEMs for TNCs. The number of firms with innovation is low. Among those firms, process innovation is higher than production innovation, and the number of innovative Thai-own firms is more or less the same as the number of innovative joint ventures (with foreign partners). On expenditures for innovation-related activities, these innovating firms spend much more on the acquisition of machinery and external knowledge than internal R&D. This reflects the nature of latecomer firms, in

Table 7.1 Structure of Thai electronic industry

	Assemblers	Part suppliers
Local firms	43%	60%
Foreign/joint venture	57%	40%
Total	100%	100%

Source: Thai Electrical and Electronics Institute

which most knowledge for their innovations come from outside. They learnt from knowledge already generated elsewhere. But they also simultaneously made their own efforts towards internal R&D to generate their own innovations and increase the capacity to absorb such external knowledge.

There are two important sub-sectors in the Thai electronic industry: semi-conductors and HDD. We will investigate the evolution of these two sub-sectors, especially the roles of key actors shaping their technological development and innovation.

7.2   Semiconductors

Currently, the semiconductor industry in Thailand accounts for one-quarter of all electronic exports (Intarakumnerd et al., 2016). Out of 2,034 firms in the Thai electronic industry, there are about three per cent of firms in semiconductor-related activities (EEI, 2012). The majority of part makers are SMEs with a substantial representation of TNCs in an assembling domain.

In the late 1980s, local Thai semiconductor enterprises, with support from a public research institute, tried to climb a technological ladder from simply assembling and packaging to process engineering development. Thailand started its R&D activity on microelectronics in 1989 by joining the Association of Southeast Asian Nations (ASEAN) – Australia cooperation project. Some very large scale integrations (VLSI) were designed in-house and sent for fabrication in Australia during the project. The microelectronic industrial infrastructure was loosely established. The further evolution of the industry, especially attempts to develop high value-added upstream sub-sectors, can be seen from the stories of three key host sites by public and private intermediaries.

National Electronics and Computer Technology Centre

With a lack of strategy and commitment at the national policy level, as the only public research institute in this field, the National Electronics and Computer Technology Centre (NECTEC) began to support Thai microelectronics by promoting IC/VLSI design and wafer fabrication, since the early 1990s. Both activities were NECTEC's own initiatives and small. Then, the cabinet approved the establishment of a wafer fabrication line for complementary metal oxide semiconductor process technology below one micrometre, with the capacity of

500 units of six-inches wafers/month in 1995. Initially, the government planned to partner with a local semiconductor enterprise by investing US$ 12 million in three years to establish the Thai Microelectronic Centre (TMEC) with a donation of US$ six million from a locally owned firm, the Alphatec Group. As a result, two wafer fabrication ventures were initiated, namely Submicron Technology Co., Ltd. and Alpha-TI Semiconductor Co., Ltd. However, both projects were heavily affected by the 1997 Asian financial crisis. An investor could not secure sufficient funds, and the projects were later cancelled. The factories built were empty, as partially installed machinery was out of order. Therefore, the machinery was confiscated by creditors. Submicron Technology's assets were acquired by NECTEC and transformed into the facility for TMEC, completed after 2000 instead. The failure to establish the first private-owned wafer fabrication facility in Thailand can be seen as a major landmark in the evolution of Thai semiconductor industry from the 1990s (Chairatana, 1997).

Compared with wafer fabrication, IC/VLSI design is not highly capital intensive. The underlying technology is still growing. There was a worldwide shortage of VLSI designers. Therefore, this was a business opportunity. Building in-house IC design capabilities became a prime innovation strategy of NECTEC. NECTEC initiated several new activities targeting IC packaging industries, HDD industries, system houses and design houses by establishing the Microelectronics Forum and graduate programmes, the IC Design Network and supporting building technological capability of local private design houses.

Thailand's Electrical and Electronics Institute

In 1998, Thailand's Electrical and Electronics Institute (Thai EEI) was established under the Ministry of Industry to become a primary organisation in enhancing the country's potential and capability to compete in the global market. Its objectives are (i) to encourage and promote the utilisation of local materials and parts for the continuous value-added production of electrical and electronics goods, (ii) to leverage international standards to improve the quality of Thai electrical and electronics products and their exports, and (iii) to be a centre in collecting, analysing, conducting research and updating information on the electronics industry, regarding production, marketing and international trade agreements. It is clear that Thai policy towards the industry prioritises downstream assembly and the development of supply chains for electrical machinery and home appliances. Interestingly, unlike the EDB of Singapore and Penang Skill Development Centre of Malaysia, the institute has also not really acted as an intermediary to facilitate knowledge flow and capability building processes between multinationals and local suppliers.

Thailand Embedded System Association

In 2001, the Thailand Embedded Systems Association (TESA) was founded by a group of academics and local private industrialists as a forum for developers and technology users in the field of embedded computing technology. TESA organises the Embedded Systems Forum as a networking space for collaboration to create opportunities and strengthen the competencies of members, to promote innovation in developing embedding systems technologies in Thailand, to develop human resources in embedded systems technology, to support the development of government technology policy related to embedded systems, and to create a positive investment environment for expanding industry. TESA members represent over 30 corporations and 30 technology solution providers and customers. They also include more than 300 individual technology developers, professors and students. The partners of TESA are 13 universities in Thailand, NECTEC and big, local and international corporates. TESA performs intermediary roles. It developed eight technology roadmaps related to the embedded systems industry for three ministries, provided testing services and certified electronic products and matched new start-ups with investors.

Attempts to strengthen upstream sub-sectors continued. In August 2004, the BOI revised conditions and incentives to stimulate interests in wafer fabrication investments by exempting import tariffs on machinery, without a time limit and exempting corporate income tax for eight years, regardless of the location and without an investment cap. Subject to approval, existing investment projects could also import machinery and equipment with duty exemption to enhance efficiency and technological capabilities. IC enterprises were incentivised to expand their activities to cover wafer processing. IC design has slowly increased, partly because the relocation to the country of foreign-specialised firms and demand from the HDD industry at home. There are three universities with strong research programs in this area – Chulalongkorn University and KMITL in Bangkok, and Chiang Mai University in Chiang Mai.

With the above attempts to go upstream, the sector still lags behind other countries in designing and testing IC, transistors, capacitors, resistors, diodes and so on. The main inputs, like wafers and bonding wire, are mainly imported from abroad, while some local inputs are lead frames. Nevertheless, there are a few exceptional cases of local firms in the upstream segments of the semiconductor sub-sector.

Stars Microelectronics Thailand (SMT)

SMT is a locally owned OEM in computer, electronic equipment, automobile, communications, safety equipment and entertainment businesses. It is also a subcontractor and electronics product designer. The co-founders were an investor with a background in the rice milling industry and a university professor in industrial engineering. The company headquarters is located in Bangpa-in Industrial Estate, Ayutthaya, Thailand with sales offices in Japan, Germany, the US and Taiwan.

SMT was founded in 1995 and earned public company status in 2004, prior to being listing in the Stock Exchange of Thailand (SET) in 2009. It was one of the first companies to enjoy the privileges of free trade zone granted by the BOI of Thailand. The firm has a registered capital of 730 million Baht (21 million

US dollars). SMT is actively engaged in upstream mass production of the micro-electronics module assembly (MMA) and IC packaging, with the factory space of 25,500 square meters. The company is currently expanding its production capacity for MMA to 100 million units per year and IC packaging to 1.2 billion units per annum, with a total of 1,450 employees, including an engineering staff of more than 120 persons.

SMT's core competency is advanced electronics manufacturing services (EMS) for MMA, IC packaging and testing, based on on-site and solution-based practice provided by local engineering teams. Another core factor is operation space management that provides secure and dedicated space where clients' intellectual properties and design are protected. The executives of SMT recognise the importance of innovation, but it is not considered a priority for leveraging of firm's competitiveness. Process innovation can be observed from investment in new machines and technologies. However, once a large amount of capital is invested in a machine or an assembly line, it limits SMT production capability because one machine can only produce a certain range of products, excluding others. Therefore, process innovation is more common in this context in a bid to improve production processes, production controls and troubleshooting disciplines. In contrast, product innovation is less evident due to the limited nature of EMS or contract manufacturers, that is, producing by orders. Also the production capability is constrained by the path-dependence of invested machines. Its influence over product modification is very limited and often found at latter stages in a production line.

External sources of innovation are suppliers and clients. SMT often requests machine specifications from machine suppliers. It also has continuous cooperation with machine suppliers, through communication and technical support provided by sales representatives and research teams. One example is the case of developing a new wire bonder. Engineers from the production line provided feedback that the old wire bonder had a short life span and required the machine operator to stop the machine and change the wire bonder. With the new wire bonder, production is higher and the cost is reduced.

Alternatively, though SMT is located in the same free trade zone with its customers in the HDD industry, cooperation is rare. SMT had to increase capabilities on its own to meet the increasing demands of these customers. However, with a new business opportunity, like a rise in demand for ultra-high radio frequency identification (RFID) chips, SMT was given the chance to co-design new products. This enables SMT to cooperate with its clients with the on-site skill of manufacturing and process engineering. The company also learnt to integrate new machineries by including clients in the manufacturing process. This was a major learning event.

Silicon Craft Technology

Silicon Craft Technology (SIC) was a start-up established in 2002 by five Thai co-founders with engineering and IC design backgrounds. SIC is a leading

Thai knowledge-intensive business enterprise that values innovation and intelligence as drivers of growth. It aims to deliver high-quality products compatible with world standards and regulations. The firm was the prime mover in an integrated circuit (IC) design in Thailand. It had the ambition to make itself a showcase of local technopreneurship, encouraging locals to join the IC design business.

Managing Director and Co-Founder Manop Thamsirianunt used to work as an analogy design engineer and IC design manager for semiconductor firms in Silicon Valley. Through a reverse brain drain scheme, he returned to Thailand in 2001 and became the head of the Thailand IC Design Incubator (TIDI), a unit of the NECTEC. Some other co-founders had doctoral degrees in engineering and were university professors.

SIC is a business ranging from state of the art, customised and standard microchips designed for RFID applications. The core competence of SIC are its experience and expertise in the design and development of world-class foundry semiconductor manufacturers of linear and mixed-signal ICs.

SIC today has succeeded in gaining more than 20 international customers for chip design and solutions from Australia, the US, Europe and Japan. The majority of employees earn engineering or related degrees from leading Thai and international universities. There are 65 active employees at SIC, almost half of them with master's degrees or doctorates (M. Thamsirianunt, personal communication, July 25, 2013). SIC provides scholarships to potential students in the leading microelectronic departments of universities and later recruits them as employees.

In the early stage of the firm's establishment, the idea of IC design in Thailand was considered a high risk and far-fetched ambition. It was very difficult for co-founders to persuade local investors to support this business. Mr. Manop, therefore, decided to leave TIDI and set up his own IC design company with other co-founders. Some co-founders continued their work as university professors, while others worked as full-time directors at SIC.

In the first six months, the new company had hardly any customers, as customers were not familiar with and did not trust the Thai IC design company. The second strategy was, therefore, to get Thai technological and IC design capabilities recognised in domestic and international markets. The company painstakingly focused only on IC design to develop chip products to sell to reputed international customers. This strategy was successful. SIC developed application-specific IC chips used in electronic devices and RFID chips that were sold in many countries. The company became internationally recognised as a chip provider.

Public procurement from NECTEC to develop a smart RFID chip used for animal identification, which SIC claimed as the world's tiniest chip with the lowest price, can be seen as an important 'learning event' for the company to gain technological and innovative capabilities. SIC also received financial investment from One Asset management, a leading Thai VC, for this IC design development.

Strategically, SIC conducts technology road mapping to segment new technologies and markets based on performance, applications and users. SIC benchmarks product performance with world IC manufacturers, like Philips, Texas Instruments and EM Microelectronics. Currently, all the company's chip products are exported. Nonetheless, after a long period of marketing efforts, local customers have begun to show interest.

7.3   Hard disk drive (HDD)

Thailand has been one of large manufacturing bases of HDD in the world since 2005, with a market share of approximately 42 per cent of the global market. In 2012, the industry contained more than 50 manufacturers producing HDD parts and employed more than 200,000 workers. Currently, two HDD producers, Seagate and Western Digital (WD), are the leading players in Thailand. The industry attempts to move away from a production-based site to one with more technologically sophisticated activities. The foreign HDD producers initiate new knowledge and product designs at their headquarters. The HDD parts manufacturers in Thailand produce parts; meanwhile, the affiliates of foreign HDD producers assemble and export products to markets worldwide. In general, the industry has built and accumulated knowledge and technologies about the production process over time until it can design and develop technologies and methods to solve problems on production and automation processes. The industry unavoidably relies on technology and knowledge transfers from the affiliates of foreign HDD producers. Two intermediary organisations played important roles in technology upgrading of the industry: IDEMA and HDDI.

International Disk Drive Equipment and Materials Association (IDEMA)

The HDD network was set up in 1999 to provide opportunities to improve local technological capability developments. In 1999, four TNCs – Seagate, Hitachi, WD and Fujitsu – established the Thailand branch of an international industrial association, namely the IDEMA, to mutually develop human resources and share information about global trends of the HDD market.

Hard Disk Drive Institute (HDDI)

In August 2004, IDEMA worked with NSTDA, a leading local research institute, to set up a cluster management organisation. Its steering committee comprises CEOs of the four TNCs, local research institutes and representatives of key governmental organisations, like the BOI. The organisation, later named HDDI, was led by a technopreneur-cum-professor who used to work for the industry and understood its needs. This organisation aimed to upgrade the capabilities of the entire industry by providing joint training programmes and collaborative R&D projects. The training courses focus on skills and knowledge critical for technology upgrading. Under HDDI's management, Thai engineers and researchers, even those not directly employed by TNCs, have been sent for 1.5-year training at the headquarters of TNCs, like WD in the US. On returning, they organised training courses for other Thai engineers and researchers and helped TNCs set up R&D laboratories in Thailand. This was the first step in changing Thailand from a production base to an R&D base for TNCs, although R&D was initially aimed at upgrading the production process rather than developing any new product.

With financial support and coordination by HDDI, industry/university cooperative research centres – that specialise in HDD components, advanced HDD manufacturing and data storage technology and applications – have been set up at Konkaen University, KMITL and KMUTT. These centres created research networks of professors and researchers in these specific fields. HDDI provided research funding through these centres. Industrial relevance is the prime concern of their research. Before submission, all research proposals must be certified by private companies.

Under HDDI, some relationships between TNCs and Thai universities have changed from short-term, technologically unsophisticated and personal to long-term, technologically advanced and institutional. WD collaborated with Suranaree University to devise a new curriculum for a special engineering bachelor's degree programme focusing on HDD technologies. WD then employed the programme's graduates. In their third year, students enrolled in the programme also received 75 per cent of the salary that would be paid to a graduate (Intarakumnerd and Chaoroenporn, 2013).

Several collaborative research projects have been launched under the three industry–university cooperative research centres supported by HDDI. For example, the development of an optical system to measure laser spot size reduction of a flying height tester (funded by Seagate), control and automation research unit (funded by Seagate), development of an algorithm for read/write hard disk head inspection using digital image processing phase 2 (funded by WD), design and development of automation production for head stack assembly (partially funded by WD) and automation (funded by Seagate).

HDDI is also trying to assist Thai suppliers (mostly SMEs) in participating in the global value chain of TNCs. It provides training courses for Thai firms which were unable to qualify as suppliers of TNCs. The courses focus on critical skills, such as automation, to meet TNCs' requirements. Thus, HDDI has tried to enhance spillover impacts from TNCs and absorptive capacities of Thai firms and non-firm actors. Its role as an 'intermediary' facilitating interaction and collective learning in the HDD sub-sector is remarkable and unique. The most significant contribution was human resource development for the Thai HDD industry. Between 2006 and 2009, a network of 15 universities was set up; two testing labs were established; an HDD technology training centre was co-founded by HDDI and WD (21,736 people joined); and 644 scholarships for HDD technology study were distributed to 202 bachelor's, 412 master's and 30 doctoral degree students. As of September 2014, 517 students had graduated, although only 144 entered the HDD industry (Sutthijakra and Intarakumnerd, 2015).

7.4 Conclusion

Though the electronic industry is the largest industry in terms of exports, the industry is generally characterised by passive technological learning. A sector-specific promotion agency, namely, Thai EEI, provided overall sectoral policy framework and master plans for the long-term development of the industry. For the semiconductor sub-sector, a public research institute like NECTEC, especially its subsidiary TMEC, offered 'specific' technological and management training, necessary grant and equity investment. A private intermediary, in the form of an industrial association, namely TESA, facilitates networking formation, builds trust among key players, and provides specific technical standard and training. However, these efforts are inadequate to move the semiconductor sub-sector to high value-added upstream activities. Only some remarkable firms have made significant attempts to upgrade their positions in the regional value chain from OEM to ODM. IC packaging is a key activity, while a small number of firms are actively engaged with IC design. There is also the emergence of an exceptional local fabless design intensive company that is capable of serving demanding global customers. These firms became successful because, unlike most local firms, they made relentless efforts to deepen their technological capabilities, leveraging external knowledges and taking risks in pursuing new markets based on their innovative products and processes.

The HDD sub-sector is more successful at technological upgrading. IDEMA, a sub-sector-specific private intermediary, imitated networking and information sharing between key stakeholders at the initial stage. The work was subsequently carried on by HDDI, established under the largest public research institute, NSTDA. HDDI deepened collaboration by jointly educating sector-specific human resources and launching R&D projects relevant to technological upgrading of leading firms in the sector.

8 Thai automotive industry

8.1 Overview of the automotive industry in Thailand

The automotive industry in Thailand started in the early 1960s under an import substitution policy and a revision of the investment promotion law to encourage automotive assembly in Thailand. The automotive industry has significantly and increasingly contributed to the Thai economy in terms of value added and employment, especially since 2001. The data from the National Economic and Social Development Board shows that total labour employed in the auto industry was about 310,000 persons, and the industry account for 10 per cent of the total value added to the country in 2015.

Thailand's automotive sector has become a part of the global production network of many car manufacturers. Completely Built Unit (CBU) vehicles and completely knocked-down (CKD) kits are produced by locally based suppliers and have been a major export product since 2000. Automobile production in Thailand surpassed one million units in 2005, and in 2010, the annual production of one-ton pickup trucks exceeded one million units for the first time. In 2011, domestic production and exports dropped because of two natural disasters, a tsunami in Japan and flooding in Thailand. Nevertheless, production and sales in Thailand recovered quickly. Domestic production, domestic sales and exports reached their peaks at 2.4 million units, 1.4 million units and 1.02 million units in 2012, respectively. As the Thai and world economies slowed down, the production, sales and exports drop to 1.9 million, 7.7 million and 1.2 million units, respectively, in 2016. According to the International Organisation of Motor Vehicle Manufacturers (OICA), Thailand is the largest producer of car in ASEAN, followed by Indonesia (1.2 million units) and Malaysia (600,000 units).

Currently, firms in the industry can be classified into three groups: 17 car assemblers, approximately 648 first-tier suppliers, and around 1,700 second- and third-tiers suppliers, which includes supporting companies. Most are small and medium-sized companies. Most assemblers are subsidiaries of TNCs. They are dominated by Japanese TNCs and the entry of the big three US car companies, namely DaimlerChrysler, General Motors and Ford, whose prime objective is to produce and export one-ton pickups from Thailand. Due to a sufficient pool

Table 8.1 Number of automotive OEM part suppliers, classified by part

Group of part	Thai	Thai majority	Foreign majority	Total
Engine parts	20	8	35	63
Electrical parts	15	10	27	52
Drive/transmission	17	6	29	52
Suspension/brake	13	1	21	35
Body parts	57	17	47	119
Accessories	18	2	19	39
Others	214	24	111	349
Total	**354**	**68**	**287**	**709**

Source: Thailand Automotive Institute

of qualified engineers and technicians and an extensive supplier network enabling integrated production, Thailand is clearly the strongest automotive production base in Southeast Asia. Nonetheless, indigenous Thai suppliers are mainly in 'non-functional' parts, such as body parts, accessories and other parts, while foreign suppliers are concentrated in the group of 'functional' parts, requiring higher manufacturing and design capabilities to produce, such as engines, electrical transmissions and suspension parts (See Table 8.1)

We will apply the concept of sectoral innovation system (see Chapter 1 for an explanation) to analyse the experiences in technological upgrading of the sector.

8.2 Roles and capabilities of key actors in Thailand's automotive industry

The key actors in the Thai automotive sector include carmakers and their component suppliers, government policy and promotion agencies, research institutes, universities (with specialised automotive industry programmes), automotive sector industrial associations, private sector technology promotion agencies, and others.

Carmakers and suppliers

Automotive firms in Thailand can be classified into three groups: assemblers, first-tier automotive part suppliers and second- and third-tier automotive sub-part suppliers. Second- and third-tier manufacturers supply raw materials and automotive sub-parts to first-tier manufacturers, who produce major automotive parts and modules before supplying to automotive assemblers, who manufacture for domestic consumption and exports.

Group 1: automotive assemblers

Currently, there are 17 assemblers. All assemblers are subsidiaries of TNCs or joint ventures. With the presence of most major carmakers, Thailand has already become one of key production bases among global players from Japan, the US and Europe. Before the 2000s, these carmakers only produced in Thailand, while more sophisticated activities like design and R&D were done in their home countries. Since the 2000s, the investment strategies of TNCs in the automotive industry have started to change, as they have begun to invest in more technologically sophisticated activities in Thailand, such as advanced engineering, process and product design and advanced testing and validation. Several major automotive TNCs (mostly Japanese) have set up technical centres in Thailand, separated from their normal production plants (for example Toyota Motor Asia Pacific Engineering and Manufacturing Co., Ltd.; Nissan Technical Center Southeast Asia Co., Ltd.; ISUZU Technical Center Asia Co., Ltd.; and Honda R&D Asia Pacific Co., Ltd.). The R&D activities of these companies began by focusing on the modification of previously designed products to fit local demands and to exploit local advantages, such as analysis of appropriate local natural raw materials and parts to meet international standards or the standards of importing countries such as the European Union's regulations. Nonetheless, there is a trend for more advanced product design to be carried out in Thailand.

The numbers of automotive parts manufacturers are around 2,289 firms, which can be classified into two groups (Group 2 and Group 3).

Group 2: direct suppliers or OEM suppliers (first tier)

This group consists of 648 auto part manufacturers who manufacture and directly supply auto parts to auto assemblers. In total, 458 auto part manufacturers are producing parts for car assemblers, and the remaining 190 auto part manufacturers are making parts for motorcycle assemblers. Among first-tier suppliers, they can be classified into six groups according to the types of automotive parts. Most Thai-owned firms concentrate on non-functional parts, namely, body parts, accessories and other parts. Being a first-tier part supplier requires rather high technological capabilities and proactive learning. Hence, there is little evidence of local firms transitioning from lower tiers to the first tier. On the other hand, several local first-tier suppliers dropped down to the second tier because they could not cope with constant demands from carmakers to design and manufacture technologically demanding parts by themselves without receiving blue print at reduced prices.

It is noteworthy to examine a case of Daisin, a primarily Thai-owned supplier, which managed to maintained status as a first-tier supplier for several decades. The company was established in 1979 to manufacture aluminium casting parts for the automotive industry as a foreign joint venture with Nissin Kogyo Co., Ltd (Thai partner was a major shareholder with 67 per cent ownership). The case of Daisin demonstrates the necessity of 'active' investment for indigenous technology capability development (not passively relying on assistance from foreign partners and other Thai firms) and the significance of working closely with suppliers and carmakers (Honda Motor Thailand) to gain support for capability developments.

The story begins with the company hiring a retired Japanese engineer. This engineer helped the company improve its production capability and negotiate with Nissin to significantly lower royalty fees. Later, the company also acquired external knowledge in addition to the partnership with Nissin by hiring other Japanese technical consultants to help develop its own design capability (in fact, Nissin was quite reluctant to help). Eventually, the company could work closely with customers (carmakers) to suggest a new design for a hand brake and a new lighting system. Honda and Toyota invited Daisin's engineers to Japan as their guest engineers to jointly develop a new brake. Daisin has now become an 'own design manufacturer' (ODM) for several carmakers. The company used its design capability from being an ODM in the automotive industry to diversify their products into other markets such as long-tail boats, small rice millers and woodcutting machines. These businesses provide much higher profit margins to the company, as it does not have to be constrained by the global production network of Japanese carmakers.

Group 3: indirect suppliers or raw material suppliers (second- and third-tier)

This group includes raw material suppliers and subcontractors for the first-tier suppliers. There are 1,641 indirect suppliers which can be classified as follows.

1   Supporting the industry with raw materials and sub-assembly parts such as leather, plastic, rubber, steel and iron, electrical and electronics parts, glass, painting and surface treatment.
2   Supporting the industry with manufacturing or equipment, for example mould & die, jig & fixture, forging, casting, tooling, cutting, surface treatment, heat treatment, precision, electronic connector and engineering plastic.

These indigenous Thai part suppliers have low technological capabilities and are largely dependent on technology provided by JV partners or licensers, but they also cannot absorb the transferred technology due to a lack of skilled labour (Brooker Group, 2002, pp. 2–14). In addition, the College of Management, Mahidol University (2006) has examined the technological capabilities of six groups of automotive component suppliers, namely, suspension and brake, interior, exterior, engine and electronic and drive transmissions. Their results show that, in general, component suppliers in Thailand could be classified into two categories based on the level of technological capabilities. Those in suspension and brake, interior and exterior had relatively higher capabilities. They have the potential to compete regionally and internationally. The other three in engine, electronics and drive transmission components have lower capabilities, since their underlying technologies are more sophisticated and required proprietary knowledge that belongs to TNCs.

Government: policy and sector-specific promotion agency

Thai government policies concerning the automotive industry can be divided into three phases.

A.   Phase I: import substitution regime

The automotive industry in Thailand started in the early 1960s under an import substitution policy and a revision of the investment promotion law to encourage automotive assembly in Thailand. During 1961–1969, nine assembly plants were set up as joint ventures between Thai and foreign carmakers. To boost investments in the domestic production of automotive parts, in 1969, the Thai government imposed a minimum local content requirement of 25 per cent on automotive assembly. After the requirement was enacted, carmakers had to start purchasing locally. However, Japanese carmakers could not rely on locally owned Thai firms, and they requested affiliated Japanese automotive parts suppliers to build plants locally and supply them.

In the late 1970s, to reduce the trade deficit and boost the industry, a localisation policy was formulated. In addition to import bans and raising tariff rates on CKD and CBU, the Thai government limited the number of automotive models and increased the local content requirement from 25 per cent to 50 per cent for passenger cars. Since the Thai automotive industry suffered low demand for cars in the early 1980s, the carmakers preferred in-house production to subcontracting for casting machine activities, and they produced automobiles themselves to utilise their excess production capacity. To further boost the development of the parts industry, the government raised the local content requirement to 54 per cent for passenger cars and 60–72 per cent for pickup trucks. This policy provided opportunities for local firms to become suppliers of TNCs in global production networks. The policy was initiated with consultation with foreign carmakers and part suppliers and implemented with a relatively high degree of flexibility.

B.   Phase II: massive FDI inflow and export promotion

FDI inflows in the automotive industry were more or less unchanged from 1970–1985, with annual inflows amounting to less than US$5 million. However, during the period 1986–1995, the annual average value of inflows increased dramatically. In the late 1980s, the appreciation of the Japanese Yen pushed up the cost of major automotive parts imported from Japan. The Yen appreciation triggered the relocation of Japanese parts producers to Thailand to reduce production costs. As indicated by the huge increase in FDI inflows, the increased TNCs involvement in the Thai automotive industry occurred for both carmakers and parts suppliers. Following their customers, Japanese parts suppliers established new affiliates for manufacturing new and more sophisticated parts since the late 1980s, when Japan experienced dramatic currency appreciation. Beyond the currency issue, compared to its neighbours, Thailand was chosen because of its advantages in geography, readiness of logistical infrastructure, availability of technicians and engineers, more liberal investment policies (having no national car projects) and more attractive business and living conditions.

Since the mid-1990s, there have been several world-class non-Japanese multiple-parts manufacturers such as Dana, TRW Steering & Suspension, Visteon Thailand, Johnson Controls, Delphi Automotive Systems and Tenneco Automotive that have established their factories in Thailand. From 1994–1997, the value of BOI promoted projects was four times higher than the records value in the period 1990–1993. The increased foreign investment in the automotive industry brought in new lines of automotive parts not previously produced in Thailand (such as transmission systems). During this period, the Thai government also assigned one-ton pickup trucks as the 'product champion' of the automotive industry. Tax incentives and other promotions were specially implemented, leading to remarkable investment and subsequent exports of this product. Thailand has become the second largest production base of pickup trucks after the US.

C. *Phase III: liberalisation and technological upgrading*

Thailand faced economic crisis in 1997. To help affected companies improve their liquidity positions, the BOI removed restrictions on foreign shareholding in November 1997. Prior to this, the policy required the majority ownership to be held by a Thai national. Many investors, mostly Japanese, took advantage of this new policy. From November 1997 to September 2000, foreign partners in 164 automotive firms changed the shareholding structure from minor shares to majority share (Charoenporn, 2001). FDI inflows in the Thai automotive industry further increased after the 1997 financial crisis and reached the record high by 2007.

In 2004, the BOI has substantially changed its policy by paying more attention to issues underlying long-term competitiveness of the country, namely, the development of indigenous technological capability and human resources. A special investment package promoting "Skill, Technology and Innovation or STI" was initiated. Firms can enjoy one or two years pf extra tax incentives if they perform the following activities in the first three years: spending on R&D or designing at least 1–2 per cent of their sales, employing scientists or engineers with at least bachelor's degree as at least 5 per cent of their workforce, investments in training employees of at least 1 per cent of their total payroll, and spending at least one per cent of total payroll on training personnel of their local suppliers.

In the late 2000s, after a long period of consultation and negotiation with industry, the economical and ecology friendly car or 'eco-car' was selected as the second product champion. Very preferential incentives, together with significant requirements to produce four out of five engine components locally, were given to interested carmakers. This new product champion is a part of the *Master Plan for Automotive Industry (2012–2016)* which aims to establish Thailand as a global *green* production base. As a result, Thailand has become the hub of eco-car production in Asia. Nissan's March and Honda's Brio, for example, have been produced and exported to the global market from production bases in Thailand.

Along with the aforementioned government policies, the Thailand Automotive Institute (TAI) was established by a cabinet resolution on July 7, 1998 to strengthen cooperation between the government and private enterprises and enhance the competitiveness of the Thai automotive industry. As a result, TAI is a *sector-specific promotional and intermediary agency* for the automotive industry. Administratively, TAI is not a part of the national bureaucracy, but it comes under the Industry Development Foundation set up by the Ministry of Industry. Therefore, the organisation's administration is rather flexible. It is not subject to the rules and regulations of ordinary government agencies and state enterprises. TAI's governing committee, headed by the Permanent Secretary of Industry, comprises representatives from the government, private sector and academia. TAI provides data, training, consultancy and testing and calibration services to firms, especially local parts suppliers.

Universities and research institutes

Key universities with active roles in helping the automotive industry in Thailand include Chulalongkorn University, KMITL, KMUTT, KMITNB and the Thai–Nichi Institute of Technology. After Thailand became a production hub, these universities started automotive engineering programs to produce qualified human capital for the thriving industry.

Chulalongkorn University is the first university in Thailand to offer a degree in automotive engineering. The department was established in 1996. Since 2005, the department has offered a master's degree in automotive engineering. The program accepts around 50 undergraduate students per year. KMITL is one of the top universities in engineering and was established in 1960. KMITL offers bachelor's, master's and doctorate degrees in engineering in many majors. For the bachelor's degree, automotive engineering is embedded in the mechanical engineering program. However, KMITL offers a separate master's degree in automotive engineering, with collaboration with the Tokyo Institute of Technology and NSTDA.

KMUTT has two departments related to the automotive industry: a mechanical engineering department and tools and a materials engineering department. The mechanical engineering department has 30 professors, of which five professors are directly involved in automotive industry. The Tools and Material Department has stronger linkages with the automotive industry than the Mechanical Engineering Department because the knowledge and experience in the department about moulding is valuable to industry.

KMUTNB offers a master's degree in automotive engineering through the Sirindhorn International Thai-German Graduate School of Engineering (TGGS). This programme is a joint programme with Rheinisch-Westfälische Technische Hochschule (RWTH) of Aachen University in Germany. RWTH is the leading Germen institute in the area of automotive engineering and closely collaborates with companies like BMW, DaimlerChrysler, Siemens and Asian and American automotive manufacturers. The automotive engineering program at TGGS was started in 2004 with a focus on industrial R&D practices and modern manufacturing processes. The curriculum is designed by RWTH Aachen University.

The Thai–Nichi Institute of Technology (TNI) was established in 2005 to educate people with specialised technological knowledge to work in Thai industries. The bachelor's degree in engineering offers majors in automotive engineering, production engineering and computer engineering. For the automotive engineering major, the course structure is developed from a Japanese Automotive Engineering course structure and from Chulalongkorn University. TNI also offers Japanese courses to its students. The programme focuses on practice-based work. TNI is planning to open a doctoral programme in future.

As for research institutes, the largest in Thailand is NSTDA. NSTDA developed the 'Automotive Cluster Program' in 2003 to enhance the competitiveness of the industry. The automotive cluster program has around 30 full-time equivalent employees. Most of the staff are mechanical engineers. Ten of them hold doctorates; however, they are in the middle and top management positions. NSTDA has partnered with TAI, Chulalongkorn University, Thammasat University, KMUTNB, KMUTT and KMITL. NSTDA has worked with the automotive industry through training, consulting service and research. NSTDA provides training and consulting services in finite element analysis to Toyota and second- and third-tier local auto part manufacturers. NSTDA also carries out the research on the intelligent traffic system, which aims to increase the driving safety and efficiency. Furthermore, NSTDA received a contract from Toyota to research how to make interior parts from natural materials.

Private sector industrial associations

There are five concerned industrial associations in the Thai automotive industry. Two of them are under the Federation of Thai Industries (FTI), and the one that specifically aims to strengthen the capabilities of indigenous suppliers is the Thai Auto Parts Manufacturers Association (TAPMA). It was created in 1978 as an association of auto parts manufacturing companies. It aims to serve as the central voice for auto parts industrialists in the country to protect, support and develop Thai industries. Currently, TAPMA has 528 companies on the membership list. They consist of all firms in the automotive parts and related industries, from third tier to first tier. TAPMA was also created to detect and address problems that hinder the development of the automobile industry in terms of production technology efficiencies, raw material import difficulties and workforce challenges, especially attracting and developing skilled labourers and engineers. In practice, TAPMA is more like a lobbyist group, seeking favour from the government. Its role as intermediary, connecting members to other actors in the automotive sector, is rather limited (Intarakumnerd and Chaoroenporn, 2013).

Private sector technology promotion agency

Established in 1973 with financial support from Japan, the TPA (Thailand–Japan) is the most successful private sector technology promotion agency (as mentioned in Chapter 3). It provides consulting services under the name 'Shindan sha Programme' to medium and large-sized local firms. The majority of the consulting projects are done with Department of Industrial Promotion as the direct customer. The department assigns the TPA to provide consulting services to local SMEs in Thailand to improve their productivity and efficiency. The type of consulting mainly uses Shindan (industrial doctors) to diagnose the problems faced by a company and subsequently arrange further problem-solving projects if the firm wants them.

8.3   Linkages and learning by interactions between key actors

There are three primary types of linkages and interactive learning in the sector: carmakers with suppliers, firms with universities and research institutes and firms with government agencies.

Carmaker–supplier linkages and learning

Foreign carmakers have played an important role in disseminating important technology to enhance the technological capability formation and growth of Thailand's supporting industries (Techakanont and Terdudomtham, 2004). TNCs are actively transferring technology through information sharing and advising to local suppliers. Many foreign part suppliers, especially Japanese ones, are involved with local parts suppliers through a technology licensing contract or as minor shareholders. However, they have expressed their intention to be co-owners and/or majority shareholders. Their prime objective was to take full control of the parts manufacturing operation. This tendency of strengthening their involvement with local parts suppliers has been observed since the late 1980s.

As the Thai automotive industry has become more export-oriented, the local content of locally assembled vehicles has naturally increased. To a certain extent, the increased importance of vehicle exports can be regarded as a structural change. The foreign ownership restriction was abolished at the beginning of the crisis in 1997. With majority ownership, these TNCs shareholders started implementing updated and more cutting-edge technology, together with close supervision by foreign technicians. This did not occur when these TNCs were involved through technology licensing channels or were minor and less active shareholders (Kohpaiboon, 2009). The inter-firm technology transfer has gradually changed from simple 'operational technology' to a higher level of 'process engineering technology'. According to Techakanont's research, there has been another shift towards 'product engineering capabilities' since the year 2000 (Techakanont, 2002). This coincides with new investment strategies by foreign carmakers to set up R&D or technical centres in Thailand and use the country as a regional and increasingly global hub for their specific products, such as one-ton pickup trucks and the eco-car. Nevertheless, only a few large local suppliers with long-term relationships to foreign assemblers and their own efforts in human resource and technology development, are given the opportunity for these higher-level technology transfers.

University–industry linkages and learning

Universities in Thailand play a significant role in generating basic knowledge and providing education. The relationships have been established and expanded through various forms mainly ranging from curriculum development, joint programs, student internships and cooperative research projects. However, the role of universities to help companies improve their technological capability is still limited.

A.   Curriculum development

Chulalongkorn University is a good example for this case. The university has established a close relationship with Toyota. Toyota helps draft curricula, a rather unusual practice for Thai universities. Toyota also provides both up to date equipment and instructors, especially in specific courses, for example, automotive manufacturing, which requires insightful knowledge and practical experiences. Toyota managers frequently took turns teaching classes. Other companies also established relationships with the programme, but they are not so intensive, interactive or frequent. The university has also expanded the relationship to auto part makers and suppliers. For example, several automotive paint firms were invited to send their employees to teach a paint-related subject.

   Corresponding to the recent investment in design and development activities of Japanese TNCs in Thailand, the teaching content has lately changed from production engineering to focus more on knowledge and skills for design and development. So there was a co-evolution of what is taught at the university and what is going on in the industry, which do not usually happen in Thai universities. However, the relationships with those firms are mainly for education. The research collaboration is still very limited and focused on the development of new materials.

B.   Student internships

A few universities have student internships with automotive firms. For example, KMUTNB has a master's degree programme in automotive engineering. The programme develops a relationship with the automotive industry through the student internships and faculty research and consulting projects. Through the internships, students can develop their thesis topic. The faculty is expected to do research and provide consultation services as part of the job requirements. An example of consultation projects is the efficient measurement of particular additives used to reduce oil consumption.

C.   Collaborative research projects

Collaborative research is still limited. Nonetheless, there are a few examples. KMITL has explored the relationship with the automotive industry through the annual Student Formula SAE Competition organised by the Society of Automotive Engineers in Thailand (SAE) to encourage students' interests in designing racing cars. During the development of racing cars, students from the automotive club worked closely with many firms in the automotive industry and received financial support. The key sponsors are Suzuki and Cobra. Also, KMITL helped modify the Suzuki engine to operate with 100 per cent ethanol at a low temperature. Cobra manufacturers carbon fibre surfboards and windsurfs. KMITL uses carbon fibre sponsored by Cobra to design auto parts for a racing car using computer-aided design (CAD). The knowledge and experience KMITL students gained was also shared with Cobra staff. As a result, Cobra can develop new products from carbon fibre, such as steering wheels.

At KMUTT, the Tools and Material Department conducted research projects in collaboration with first-tier local part suppliers as PhD students' research. The research topics of these students come from problems faced by these part suppliers. In general, these first-tier part suppliers support research by providing materials and infrastructure. The financial support usually comes from government agencies in the form of scholarships and research funding. The department also works with second- and third-tier suppliers through the master thesis and undergraduate senior projects.

Firms–government linkages and learning

The key linkages here are the links between firms and the TAI. Though TAI has different roles and activities as mentioned earlier, the most important to private firms is the Automotive Human Resource Development Programme (AHRDP) during 2006–2011. This programme was a joint collaboration between Thailand and Japan. In addition to TAI, the FTI also joined the programme. The Japanese side was led by the JICA, the Japan External Trade Organisation and the Japanese Chamber of Commerce. The programme aimed to upgrade the capability of local auto part manufacturers. Its mission focused on enhancing

Thai automotive workforce capabilities. At the end, graduates of the programme should be able to train other people in their companies or at their supplier partners. Four leading Japanese companies participated in the programme by providing training experts and course materials in their specialised area; Toyota (Toyota Production System), Honda (mould and die technology), Nissan (scheme of skill improvement), and Denso (manufacturing skill and mind management). The training covered theoretical knowledge, hand-on skills and attitude improvement. Thai university professors were also invited to teach in theoretical courses. The auto part manufacturers (either foreign-owned, joint venture or local firms) were invited to send qualified persons to participate in the programme. Executives of these companies were asked to show their commitment by opening up to students for knowledge and skills sharing and taking turns to host other companies in factory visits. This is a remarkable programme. It has created a pool of talented trainers and has improved awareness of the importance of human resource development in the sector. However, the results, in terms of the actually upgrading the Thai automotive workforce, are ambiguous. Some companies, especially larger ones, set up training centres or training courses after joining AHRDP. Uptake was less enthusiastic for smaller companies.

The second phase of the human resource development programme organised by TAI started in 2013 under the Japan–Thai Economic Partnership Agreement. It is called the Automotive Human Resource Development Institute Programme. Training in this phase concentrates on higher knowledge and skills than in the first phase. They include advanced technology development activities like R&D (especially, value added and value engineering), Toyota Production System and Manufacturing Preparation. Every year, six to seven Japanese experts (mostly retired engineers from leading car manufacturers and first-tier suppliers) were sent to Thailand to train 10 Thai 'master trainers' who were employees of Thai and foreign first-tier part makers in Thailand. These Thai master trainers are expected to train 100 'trainers' who are working for first- and second-tier part makers. These trainers are supposed to train their colleagues (the so-called 'trainees') in their own companies. In total, the project aims to produce 300,000 trainees within 10 years. This is very ambitious. In practice, the Japanese experts were reluctant to transfer real technology. The training of master trainers was too short, and it was inadequate, in terms of genuine practice. There was also no mechanism to ensure and incentivise trainers to subsequently train their co-workers in their companies (Atthawit Techawiboonwong, director of Auto Parts Manufacturer Department, TAI, personal communication, December 20, 2014).

8.4 Conclusion

Thailand's automotive industry has a long history, over 50 years. It has come a long way from a small import substituting industry to a large and vibrant exporting one. It contributes significantly and increasingly to the country's GDP and employment.

Looking more closely, we can also observe three main evolution patterns of the Thai automotive sectoral innovation system. Firstly, the system is evolving from a passive learning and fragmented system to a more active learning and coherent one. Foreign carmakers, first-tier suppliers and several local suppliers made considerable effort to enhance their technological and innovative capabilities. Universities and research institutes started to have sector-specific teaching and research programmes and closer collaboration with the industry. The sector-specific government promotion agency (i.e., TAI) has been increasingly acting as an 'intermediary' organisation, establishing and strengthening linkages between foreign firms, local suppliers, universities and other government agencies. The long-standing institutional obstacles, especially the attitude of technologically passive learning of Thai suppliers, have also been considerably improved.

Secondly, the results of this change enable the system to gradually upgrade from a 'production' system to an 'innovation' and 'R&D-intensive' one. Foreign carmakers and first-tier suppliers, together with selected Thai first-tier and leading second-tier suppliers, began to set up R&D/technical centres separate from the production departments. As a result, they have been seeking more 'innovation/R&D-intensive' collaborations with local universities and research institutes.

Lastly, the system has increasingly become more 'product-specific'. Rather than producing and innovating varieties of vehicles, as in the past, product champions like the one-ton pickup truck and, subsequently, the eco-car have emerged in the last 15 years. These product champions have significantly increased both in terms of absolute numbers and relation to the country's total production and exports. The global car industry's market views Thailand as a specialised production and, increasingly R&D, base of these specific products.

9 Thai seafood industry

9.1 Overview of Thailand's seafood industry

Thailand has become one of the world's largest and most advanced producers and exporters of processed food products. Its profound agricultural traditions and abundance of natural resources, suitable climate for cultivation and agricultural and fishery farming, combined with significant investments in international quality standards, technology, and food safety R&D, helped Thailand attain its status as the sole net food exporter in Asia. In 2014, Thailand's exported food products generated US$30 billion. Thailand consistently ranks as a major food producer regionally and also worldwide (FAO, 2016).

In the seafood industry in particular, Thailand is one of the main players in the world. In 2014, the value of fish exports reached US$6.5 billion. This makes Thailand the fourth largest fish exporter in the world, behind China, Norway and Vietnam. Thailand is also an important market in Asia. Its imports were valued at around US$2.7 billion in 2014. During the last decade, there has been a great deal of expansion in the frozen shrimp and cephalopod processing industries and in tuna canneries. Thailand is now the world's biggest producer and exporter of canned tuna and shrimp. In 2013, the export value of canned tuna was US$ 2.5 billion, while other canned and processed seafood exports accounted for nearly US$ 5 billion (FAO, 2016).

Domestic raw materials, on the other hand, have been decreasing for the past decade due to declines in marine capture fisheries and aquaculture; in particular, the shrimp industry has been facing disease-related problems in recent years. Thailand has huge seafood processing capacity and, at the same time, growing domestic demand due to increases in the disposable income of local consumers. Thailand imports seafood raw materials from all over the world, and these imports are expected to increase further in the years to come.

The value chain of the seafood industry can be divided into three levels:

1   Upstream: sourcing and production of raw materials, which can come from the sea or farming
2   Midstream: post-harvesting, sales, transportation and early processing
3   Downstream: processing, product development, freezing and exporting

Processed seafood has a higher value per kilogram than chilled or frozen seafood. More than 90 per cent of Thai seafood products are exported; the majority of these exports are chilled or frozen shrimp. More than 90 per cent of Thai exports are made-to-order products (also known as OEMs) for foreign customers. Thai-owned brands, though starting to increase considerably, are still far fewer than foreign-owned brands. Nevertheless, as Thai seafood products face competition from cheaper countries like Vietnam and Indonesia, branded and more sophisticated products are increasingly important for the future survival of the industry. Thailand has also been facing barriers in the form of increased food safety standards in developed countries. The Thai seafood industry has two major market segments: (i) chilled or frozen shrimp, and (ii) chilled or frozen fish. Both are labour-intensive and low-tech industries. More than 85 per cent of raw materials in the shrimp industry come from farming, while most of the raw materials for the fish industry are caught from waters inside and outside the country.

We will try to explain the successes and challenges of the seafood industry by investigating three components of the seafood sector innovation system: knowledge and technology, key actors and their linkages, and demand conditions and institutional factors.

9.2   Knowledge and technology

In general, the upstream processing activities are labour-intensive. Most labourers are unskilled; however, some activities like fish-filleting require skilled labour. For midstream processes, technologies (especially the freezing technologies) are neither sophisticated nor standardised. More advanced technologies are applied in the product and process design stage, new product development stage and quality control stage. These technologies can be divided into four groups.

1   Technologies related to production, namely, production process improvement, product design and development and waste management. These technologies are already in use in large firms; however, most SMEs do not possess these technologies.

2   Technologies related to industrial and health standards can be divided into three sub-categories.

   •   Quality control technologies, especially, Hazard Analysis and Critical Control Point (HACCP)[1] and Good Manufacturing Practice (GMP)[2]. These technologies are now widely implemented in both large firms and SMEs as they are strictly enforced requirements of foreign importers and, to a large extent, are promoted by Thailand's Fisheries Department.

   •   Testing and certification technologies. These are also critical for ensuring quality and safety and assessing the environmental impact of products. As these technologies are costly, only large firms have them. In addition, the availability of internationally accepted testing and quality assurance services in public laboratories is still limited. Taking advantage of these services can be time-consuming. There is also a need for testing and certifying emerging and increasingly significant food segments, namely, organic and halal food.

- Traceability technologies. These technologies are very important because customers, especially those from demanding markets like Europe, would like to monitor and control every stage of food production from the beginning to the end, that is, from 'farm to fork'. RFID tags, which enable new data to be added at every stage of production, are now widely used among large and medium Thai producers for their export products. However, small producers are lagging behind in the adoption of this technology, and RFID technologies have yet to be applied to all seafood products.

3 Food packaging technologies. New packaging technologies have been used to ensure high levels of cleanliness and freshness in processed food. These technologies also keep the taste as authentic as possible. Moreover, significant value can be added to the original products with beautiful, convenient and environmentally friendly packaging. Retort pouches, for instance, are now widely used for packaging. Other technologies like biodegradable packaging or smart packaging (which prolongs shelf life and provides more information on the products through changes in signalling colours and odours) have already been introduced. However, once again, these technologies are not widely used, as they are still too expensive and need further development.

4 Logistic technologies. New logistic technologies for the management and transportation of raw materials need to be of the highest quality (to ensure high levels of quality and freshness in seafood products) and, at the same time, cost effective. Today, domestic transportation largely depends on costly and ineffective road transportation. The rail system is underdeveloped. SMEs are also facing serious problems in accessing IT-related logistic technologies.

9.3   Key actors and their linkages

There are four groups of actors in the Thai seafood sectoral innovation system: firms, universities and public research institutes, government policymakers and supporting organisations, and private intermediary organisations. There are two kinds of seafood companies: large firms and SMEs.

Large firms

Large firms supply both domestic and export markets. Most are still OEMs producing under the brand name of large domestic supermarkets and foreign customers. However, some of them have become OBMs, for example, CP

Group, Thai Union Frozen, Surapon Food, Pacific Fish Processing (PFP), S&P, and Prantalay. The ratio of OEM to OBM products of these firms is around 1:1. Many of the large firms have received technologies from abroad through joint ventures.

Large firms have full or partial vertical integration. They perform several activities in the value chain from farming to marketing to distribution. To ensure that they will have sufficient high-quality raw materials, these firms either have their own farms or are engaged in contracted-farming with local farmers. These local farmers are supplied with larvae, necessary materials and technical support. Some firms even have large fishing fleets for sea fishing.

In the food processing stage, food technologists and engineers design new production processes and upgrade existing ones. This enables these firms to produce new products and reduce production costs. Most firms have their own R&D department to carry out product and process innovations. Typically, personnel in the R&D departments have educational backgrounds in food science and food engineering. Recently, graduates in home economics and food chefs (both domestic and international) have been hired to work in these departments and to develop (in collaboration with food scientists and engineers) new recipes for ready-to-eat and ready-to-cook products. Some firms have expanded their R&D activities by setting up culinary development centres to actively develop new processes and products with their customers, whom the firms view as the most important source of knowledge.

Working closely with the R&D departments are the marketing departments; their jobs are to find out what new products the customers need and to persuade the customers that the firm's new products meet their needs. Several firms have had product innovations in frozen or ready-to-eat food. Various recipes were developed to satisfy demanding customers with different tastes.

There are also process innovations to increase productivity, safety and traceability. In addition, the CP Group owns several regional distribution outlets, like Seven-Eleven and Lotus department stores in China. S&P, another firm, was originally a locally owned chain restaurant that specialised in Thai food. It expanded to produce packaged ready-to-eat food for the mass market under its own brand name.

Linkages with domestic and overseas customers are vital to learn about preferred technologies and styles of packaging, foreign-market regulations and consumer tastes. This is particularly important for OEM products. However, linkages with universities have become increasingly significant in recent years. These linkages take several forms, namely, joint or contracted research to develop new products through personnel training and student internships.

Small and medium enterprises (SMEs)

Like large firms, SMEs also supply both domestic and foreign markets. However, most SMEs are family businesses relying on imported technologies. Technological development activities are limited to minor adaptations to imported machinery and equipment. Most SMEs do not have efficient energy and waste management systems. Unlike large firms, which pay attention to continuous development, the quality control systems of SMEs are implemented only to the extent needed to pass minimum certification requirements. There are no R&D activities. Product and process development is passive; that is, SMEs' ambitions do not extend beyond satisfying the immediate needs of customers. Many only export standardised early-stage processed seafood, such as unpeeled shrimp (especially to Europe). Personnel training is also limited, as SMEs prefer to recruit experienced production personnel. Finally, linkages with universities and public research institutes are very limited because SMEs typically seek technical assistance from other manufacturers.

Universities and public research institutes

In general, universities and public research institutes only tend to have relationships with large firms. Further, any collaborative activities with these large firms, such as training of the firm's personnel or student internships, are short-term. In addition, the R&D activities of many universities and public research institutes are limited and out of sync with the industry's needs. There are, however, some that perform better and have more sector-specific activities. Here we will examine the roles of these universities and research institutes.

A. Kasetsart University

Two faculties have played significant roles in the Thai seafood industry: the Faculty of Fisheries and the Faculty of Agro-Industry. The Faculty of Fisheries offers degrees from the bachelor level to the PhD level. It runs teaching programmes for students and conducts research on topics including farming, process design and improvement, product development in various forms, testing and sensory technologies. It is engaged in both contracted and joint research agreements to develop new recipes with firms in the industry. Its aqua-business unit offers technical services to firms. The faculty members also have collaborative education with the industry. Some students have been sent to work as interns in the factories and laboratories of firms. These students were jointly supervised by professors and the firms' food specialists.

The Faculty of Agro-Industry teaches courses, mainly in production processes. Recently, the industry's demand for employees who can perform various functions and collaborate with people from several departments has increased. As a result, the faculty have begun to offer courses in product development and marketing. Large firms in the seafood industry contracted their research out to the faculty in several areas, such as raw materials analysis, production process improvement and product development. The university's alumni, who are now working in large firms, are important for the development of such research links between the university and industry. The main obstacle to better university–industry research collaborations is differences in time horizons between the two parties.

B.   Suan Dusit University

This university is well-known for its expertise in the food industry. It offers programmes in food science and technology, home economics and food industry and services. The food science and technology programme focuses on giving students sufficient knowledge of food properties and chemistry, processing techniques and product development to work in the food industry. The home economics programme produces chefs that are in great demand at the R&D departments of large firms. The food industry and services programme aims to produce graduates with skills in managing food-related businesses such as hotels, hospitals and bakeries. Students spend many hours working as interns in these businesses. They learn and develop skills covering the entire food value chain, including production, marketing, servicing and management. In addition to student internship programmes, the university has also collaborated with the industry in jointly developed projects to develop new products and upgrade existing ones and provided consultant services to improve production and quality-management systems, like HACCP and GMP.

C.   KMUTT

The Food Engineering Department of KMUTT is very famous for its master's degree programme, called the Food Engineering Practice School (FEPS). FEPS adopted the work-integrated learning approach. This approach mixes theory and education in the classroom with six months of practical experience in factories. Graduates are expected to be skilled in research, critical thinking, problem-solving, communication and presentation. Student theses are based on the problems and needs of the industry.

The critical success factor that differentiates FEPS from other internship programmes is that university professors are dispatched to factories and stay there with students as site directors. They teach students on-site, in collaboration with factory supervisors. As a result, FEPS's graduates are very much in demand in the food industry. In fact, some firms have provided students with scholarships and recruited them after graduation. The programme has also attracted support from government research funding organisations, such as the TRF and the NSTDA.

D.   Punyapiwat Techno Business School and Punyapiwat Institute of Management

These schools are owned and operated by the CP Group: the largest conglomerate and producer in the Thai seafood industry. They aim to educate students, at both the vocational and degree levels, under the concept of 'work-based learning'. The main programme is Modern Trade Business Management, producing especially qualified personnel for the CP Group's retail (Seven-Eleven) and wholesale (Siam Makro) businesses. However, there are other programmes specifically catering for food industry, such as Food Business Management, Food Processing Technology Management and Innovative Agriculture Management. Students switch back and forth between studying and working in the shops and factories of the CP Group and its business partners. Altogether, students in the four-year bachelor programme in the Modern Trade Business Management Programme spend two years in the classroom and two years in the workplace. This practical education is remarkable compared to normal universities. As a result of this method of education, students from these schools can work in companies after graduation without the need for extensive training by their new employers.

E. NSTDA

NSTDA is the largest public research institute in Thailand (see detailed discussion on Chapter 4). National Biotechnology Centre (BIOTEC), under NSTDA, carries out research contributing to the development of the seafood industry. Between 2001 and 2003, during the yellow head virus and white spot syndrome virus epidemics in shrimp farms across the globe, BIOTEC developed effective and inexpensive test kits that enabled farmers to detect infection at a much earlier stage and take steps to deal with that infection. As a result, the Thai shrimp industry was not as severely affected as its major competitors (Tanticharoen et al., 2008).

NSTDA's Industrial Technology Assistance Programme (ITAP) acts as an important intermediary between experts at universities and public research institutes and SMEs. The aim is to bridge the gap between the two and encourage consultancy projects to improve the technological capabilities of SMEs, especially to improve production line and quality control systems. ITAP provides 50 per cent of the financial support for the consultancy projects and monitors their progress from beginning to end.

Government policy and supporting organisations

In general, the policies of the Thai government and the organisations in charge of supporting the industry are not very effective; the latters' roles overlap too much, and coordination among them is rather poor. However, some of the agencies supporting the seafood industry perform well. Some have played important roles in upgrading the industry. This section will investigate the roles of these agencies.

A. Fisheries Department

The Fisheries Department is the main agency responsible for the formulation and implementation of policies to support the seafood industry, from the fishing and farming stage to the processing stage. It also conducts its own R&D and transfers technologies to farmers and SMEs. In addition, it provides quality certification to aquatic farms and their products. It has played a very important role in introducing and upgrading quality control systems and traceability systems to fish and shrimp farms all over the country. As a result, the chemical residues in the seafood products from Thailand have been substantially reduced. The products now meet the standards of importers in developed countries.

B.   *National Bureau of Agricultural Commodity and Food Standards (ACFS)*

ACFS was established in 2002 to enforce standards along the entire food supply chain to control agricultural food production and processing. ACFS is also charged with accrediting certification bodies for agricultural commodities and foods, negotiating with international partners to reduce non-tariff barriers to trade, and improve the competitiveness of Thai agricultural and food standards. ACFS designs and enforces standards in accordance with international frameworks such as the Food and Agriculture Organisation of the United Nations (FAO) and World Health Organisation (WHO)'s Codex Alimentarius Commission. ACFS enforces three kinds of food standard: general standards (e.g., chemical residuals), product standards (e.g., specific to frozen shrimp), and system standards (e.g., good practices in the production of aquatic products). These standards are very important for upgrading the quality of Thai seafood products. In addition, ACFS has participated in negotiations to set up new international standards that affect the competitiveness of Thai exports. Unfortunately, ACFS's ability to negotiate effectively was compromised by a lack of credible local research, which was needed to provide scientific evidence to support their position regarding standard setting.

C.   *National Food Institute (NFI)*

The NFI was established in 1996, under the Ministry of Industry, to develop the food processing industry. NFI is engaged in the following activities: (i) offering fee-based laboratory services (chemical, microbiological, and physical testing); (ii) offering consulting services related to the adoption of HACCP practices; (iii) offering training seminars and workshops, particularly related to international trade; and (iv) publishing literature on food safety and quality. NFI acts as an intermediary between firms (especially SMEs) and food industry experts who can provide research and training. It has also leveraged resources from other government agencies to support the capability development of firms. NFI conducts research related to developing policies and strategic plans for the government and on problems in the food industry. NFI initiated the first Master Plan (2002) and the second Master Plan (2008) for the Thai food industry. NFI was later selected to be the focal institute for the creation of a strategic plan for the halal food business.

D. *Thai Food and Drug Administration (Thai FDA)*

The main role of the Thai FDA is to protect the health of consumers by ensuring the safety, quality and efficacy of health products (which include food and drugs). Chilled or frozen seafood products are subject to the FDA's regulations on GMP and HACCP and require approval from the FDA before launch on the market. In addition to these regulations, there are also general regulations on the labelling of food products and specific regulations (like those on nutraceutical products) to control illicit marketing techniques and the exaggeration of the properties of those products. The FDA involved other government and private sector agencies (like the Fisheries Department, NFI, the Thai Frozen Food Association, and academics) in the process of drafting new regulations.

E. *Department of International Trade Promotion*

As Thai foods have been well recognised overseas, it is important to distinguish 'Thainess' and their quality from others. To this end, the Department of International Trade Promotion, under the Ministry of Commerce, plays an important role in launching a branding program, namely, "Thai Select" to certify and to promote authentic Thai foods or cuisines around the world. Also, the programme encourages Thai restaurateurs and Thai food producers to maintain their high product and service standards.

Regarding linkages between government actors, there was an effort to consolidate the work of relevant government agencies in the food sector, especially at the policy level. Most importantly, the "Thailand Kitchen of the World" project was co-hosted by the NFI under the Ministry of Industry with the Ministry of Agriculture and Cooperatives. The focus of the project was to incorporate Thai traditions into cooking Thai foods, using safe and residue-free local ingredients. Following series of workshops with public and private stakeholders, halal and organic foods were highlighted as the most important innovations. However, lacking clear direction and implementation strategies throughout value chains once again means that the project was not as successful as planned.

Although Thai government agencies responsible for regulating and promoting the seafood industry perform better than their counterparts in other industries, the industry still considers the overall government structure to be too complicated and too slow to respond to rapid technological and market changes. The national strategy for the food industry is still too passive to ensure the timely development and upgrade of products. Testing and quality assurance services are also slow. These problems cause a serious bottleneck in the marketing of Thai products to demanding markets. In addition, the government's engagement in international negotiation is passive, leaving Thai firms at a disadvantage to their customers and competitors.

Private sector intermediaries

Some industrial and professional associations play key roles in building trust among their members and encouraging collaboration with external agencies. They also produce 'club goods' such as industry intelligence and services that are useful for their members' activities. Here we will explore the roles of two private agencies: Thai Frozen Food Association (TFFA) and Food Science and Technology Association of Thailand (FoSTAT).

A. TFFA

TFFA is a private, non-profit organisation founded in 1968. It has more than 200 member companies. The main business of its members is the processing and exporting of frozen foods. Almost all are Thai-owned companies. TFFA has the following roles: to promote entrepreneurship in the frozen food industry, to provide consulting services, to encourage information exchange and harmony among its members, to serve as a mediator in conflicts that may occur among its members (or between members and outsiders), to establish regulations and mutual agreements for members to follow, to aid in the smooth operation of their businesses, to survey and study their members' opinions about their businesses, and to cooperate with government entities responsible for the industry. Among these roles, the consulting (on international manufacturing standards) and mediating roles are the most prominent. TFFA has had a number of successes: it has mediated conflicts between large and small members, it was successful in developing club goods, and it helped set up an endowment fund to be used to mitigate short-term common threats, such as anti-dumping measures imposed by importing countries, which is rare for Thai industrial associations. However, it has not been able to persuade its members to cooperate in solving long-term issues, such as general upgrades to the industry (Intarakumnerd and Charoenporn, 2013).

B. FoSTAT

FoSTAT is a not-for-profit professional association established in Thailand in 1976 to disseminate knowledge related to food science and technology to private and public sector entities to facilitate compliance with food laws and promote professionalism. It provides consultancy services, training and seminars to SMEs, food professionals and the general public. More importantly, it initiated the Certified Food Professional (CFoP) programme with an aim to increase the knowledge of food industrialists. Not only do candidates for the CFoP programme need to have graduated with a science degree and have work experience, they also have to pass a set of exams in food chemistry, food microbiology, food processing and engineering and food quality systems and sanitation. These CFoPs now work in many companies in the industry.

9.4 Demand conditions and institutional factors

Since the 2000s, there have been several interesting trends in demands in the food industry. These trends may have a significant impact on innovation.

1 Increasing *urbanisation* and *fast and convenient lifestyles* of urban cities encourage consumers to buy ready-to-eat, ready-to-cook and frozen food much more than before.
2 Consumers are becoming more health and environmentally conscious. *Health* food and *green* food have become popular.
3 Ironically, some urban and well-off consumers long for a slower pace of life (as it was in the past). Therefore, *slow* food (dishes that take a longer time to consume and allow the diner to relax) and *nostalgic* or *original-taste* food (as opposed to fusion food) is more appealing to these consumers.
4 The globalisation of trade, investment, and people's mindsets, in addition to the emergence of a cosmopolitan lifestyle, has made *mixed-international food* popular.
5 Ageing societies have created a new market segment for food. This niche market will be larger in the future, as the demographics of several countries shift to increasingly older citizens.

Two institutional factors shape the roles and interactions of the industry actors: (i) government policies, and (ii) regulations and industrial standards. Since the 2000s, there have been two master plans for the Thai food industry approved by the cabinet. Both plans emphasise the importance of the seafood industry. The second plan covers the period from 2010 to 2014. Apart from the overall master plans, the Fisheries Department drafted and launched several product-specific strategic plans, such as plans designed to promote shrimp or black tiger prawn production and sale. However, these plans face many problems in budget allocation, implementation, monitoring and evaluation.

The seafood industry depends a great deal on exports. Therefore, international regulations, industrial and safety standards like GMP or HACCP, and private standards imposed by major importers like the British Retail Consortium are critical factors in the successes and failures of the industry. Although these standards could be viewed as non-tariff barriers from developed countries, in actuality, they have helped Thai companies upgrade their production, quality control and traceability systems. While it is true that they created a crisis when they were first introduced and enforced in the 1990s, many Thai firms managed to upgrade their capabilities and were able to comply with the new standards. As a result, many firms became much stronger than they had been. In the future, Thai firms hope that Thai agencies, in collaboration with private firms, are able to implement more proactive policies regarding international standards. They also hope that Thai agencies will be able to protect the interests of the Thai seafood industry by actively setting international standards with support from scientific research.

9.5 Innovations in the Thai seafood industry

In the past 10 years, the Thai seafood industry has changed considerably. There have been several product, process and position innovations. Some of these innovations emerged from changing demand conditions, convergences between various scientific disciplines, convergences between science and art and convergences between manufacturing and services. Some were the results of interaction between different actors in the innovation system.

Since the beginning of the 2010s, the domestic market for processed and frozen food is considered a new and potential market associated with retail and wholesale industry for food service. The identified trends from the author's technology foresight workshop indicated that consumers will demand even healthier, greener and more convenient food, as they pay more attention to health and environmental issues while living in bigger cities and having busier lifestyles. Food will be more customised according to differences in lifestyles, age groups (e.g., food designed for babies, teenagers, and old people), health conditions and so on. Producing these types of food requires knowledge from natural science (nutraceutical science for ageing and rejuvenation, food functionality), advanced technologies (sensory technologies, and smart and biodegradable packaging), social science (food culture and diversity), and art (new recipes and food packaging design). As a result, convergence innovations will substantially increase.

Product innovation

The most remarkable product innovations were new frozen, ready-to-cook and ready-to-eat, seafood products in a range of new Oriental and Western recipes, especially

- Thai cuisine: green curry, red curry, yellow curry, fried basil (*kraprow*), rice porridge, and shrimp fried rice (based on different tastes and ingredients),
- Chinese cuisine: Chinese dumplings, egg noodle, and wanton soup,
- Japanese and Korean cuisine: teriyaki style dishes, and Korean-barbeque style dishes,
- Western cuisine: fish fillets, pizza, hamburgers and sandwiches.

Changes in demand, especially with urban and cosmopolitan lifestyles, gave rise to new opportunities. Fusion foods based on creative mixtures of different cuisines were also introduced. These new products were the results of convergences between science (new food packaging technology, new freezing and chilling technologies, and improved food logistics), art (diverse global food culture, creative and delicious recipes, artistic and attractive packaging, and interesting product storylines), and services (changes in supply chain of food service in wholesale and retail sector and advertising).

New products were mostly designed by R&D departments comprised of food scientists and food engineers, in addition to chefs and home economics graduates. Though the staff members of these R&D departments have different educational backgrounds and experiences, they have learnt to work together. Some companies recruited famous domestic or foreign chefs to head R&D centres. Some changed their departmental names to *culinary centres* to reflect the creative mix of scientific R&D and art. Cross-departmental coordination among R&D, production, engineering and marketing departments was also crucial in bringing new products to market. In the food industry, innovation is far from a linear model. There is a great deal of trial and error, and feedback from various departments is required. Some companies created more than 100 new recipes per year; however, of these, only ten or so reached the market. In the process of new product development, these firms sometimes leverage the expertise of other actors in the innovation system (especially universities and public research institutes) for products, such as licensing, or conducting collaborative research on new food packaging.

Process innovation

There have been several process innovations developed mainly by large firms, namely, production process design and engineering, new farming techniques for domesticated shrimp brood stock, shrimp feeding technique and GMP and HACCP system improvements. Certain emerging process innovations are also expected to have strong future impacts, namely, next-generation freezing technology, traceability and IT-enabling food logistics, and farmaceuticals (the application of biotechnology in agriculture farming to produce highly functional materials for food production). Large Thai firms are conducting research, sometimes in collaboration with universities, to realise these innovations.

Position innovation

Position innovation is defined as changes in the context in which the products and services are introduced (Tidd and Bessant, 2013). The most obvious position innovation, which has been adopted by several firms, is the introduction of a once-common street food in the form of a new ready-to-eat, packaged product. Street food was popular in Thailand and other developing countries. However, among middle-class people, whose income has increased as the Thai economy has progressed and whose lifestyle has become Westernised, quality and food safety is always a big concern. The seafood processing firms have recognised this opportunity. They have adapted street food recipes into ready-to-eat packaged products. This has proven to be a big success. This kind of innovation also illustrates convergence innovations based on a combination of technologies (ready-to-eat production processes and packaging) and an understanding of changes in urban society.

9.6 Conclusion

Thailand's seafood industry has experienced substantial changes in the past 30 years. It became a successful exporting industry, and it has also climbed up the global value chain. Once an exporter of unprocessed or semi-processed seafood, Thailand now exports high value-added processed frozen food in a range of recipes. Some of these products are produced under local brand names. In the domestic market, several large firms have marketed varieties of ready-to-eat, ready-to-cook, and frozen seafood products under their own brand names through their own distribution channels or those of others.

Underlying this success is an increasingly strong, coherent sectoral system of innovation. Large firms have increased their technological capabilities. Many of these firms have their own R&D departments to carry out product development. Some SMEs have also improved their capabilities. There are universities and public research institutes that have specific education and research programmes for the seafood industry. Their relationships with firms, especially large ones, have become stronger through various mechanisms, namely, joint and collaborative R&D, licensing, training, consulting and technical services. Government policy and regulating and supporting agencies have also played critical roles in upgrading the industry, especially through their increasingly strong enforcement of industrial and safety standards. Unlike other sectors in Thailand, private intermediaries (like sector-specific industrial associations) have played a crucial role in the building of trust among their member firms, upgrading the capabilities of their member firms, facilitating linkages among members and facilitating linkages between member firms and other actors in the sectoral innovation system. Changes in demand and institutional factors, such as stricter regulations, have also stimulated innovations, especially in response to the emergence of niche market segments.

This sector is a good example for convergence innovation. It has produced products, processes and position innovations. There were several product innovations, like branded ready-to-eat, ready-to-cook, and frozen products based on Thai, Oriental, Western and fusion recipes. These innovations are the results of the integration of knowledge and expertise from science, social science, art and services. They were achieved by R&D departments with personnel from various disciplines, in addition to interaction between the R&D and other departments within firms. In several cases, firms leveraged external knowledge by collaborating with local universities and public research institutes. The study finds that for the convergence of innovation to occur, firms must be proactive in their approach to acquiring and creating new knowledge in their industry. Convergence innovation also requires a strong, coherent sectoral innovation system to be in place.

However, as the new technologies and knowledge necessary for future innovation and upgrading have arrived or are about to do so (e.g., next-generation freezing technologies, nutraceuticals, new functional food, smart packaging, IT-enabled food logistics, traceability, and so on), the sector continues to face serious challenges. Thai firms need to acquire these technologies either with their own R&D or by leveraging other actors in the sectoral innovation system. At the same time, the market and society are also changing. This will give rise to new demand, for example, food for different age groups or food for more urban, environmentally friendly and health-conscious lifestyles. Regulations on food safety and environmental impact such as carbon and water footprints (particularly from developed country markets) will be stricter. Competition in seafood exports from emerging countries like Indonesia and Vietnam will be much fiercer. As a result, even more proactive learning strategies and behaviours of firms and a more coherent and even stronger sectoral innovation system are needed to ensure the future sustainability and success of the Thai seafood industry.

Notes

1 HACCP is a systematic preventive approach for food safety and biological, chemical, and physical hazards in production processes that can cause the finished product to be unsafe that also designs measurements to reduce these risks to a safe level. It was adopted by the US in the 1960s and was internationally accepted later.
2 GMP is the practice required to conform to the guidelines of agencies which control authorisation and licensing for manufacture and sale of food, drug products, and active pharmaceutical products to make sure that products are high quality and do not pose any risk to the consumer or public.

Bibliography

AIT/Asia Policy Research. (2003). 'Strengthening the Hard Disk Drive Cluster in Thailand,' Interim Report submitted to the National Science and Technology Development Agency, Bangkok, Thailand.

Aiyar, S., Duval, R., Puy, D., Wu, Y., and Zhang, L. (2013). 'Growth Slowdowns and the Middle-Income Trap,' IMF Working Paper No. 13/71, International Monetary Fund, Washington, DC.

Amsden, A. (1989). *Asia's Next Giant: South Korea and Late Industrialisation*, New York: Oxford University Press.

Amsden, A. (2001). *The Rise of the Rest: Challenges to the West From Late-Industrializing Economies*, New York: Oxford University Press.

Amsden, A. and Hikino, T. (1993). 'Borrowing Technology or Innovating: An Exploration of the Two Paths to Industrial Development,' in R. Thomson (ed.), *Learning and Technological Change*, New York: St. Martin's Press.

Amsden, H. and Chu, W. (2003). *Beyond Late Development: Taiwan's Upgrading Policies*, Cambridge, MA: MIT Press.

Anderson, B. (1977). 'Withdrawal Symptoms: Social and Cultural Aspects of the October 6 Coup,' *Bulletin of Concerned Asian Scholars* 9(3): 13–30.

Ariffin, N. and Bell, M. (1997). 'Patterns of Subsidiary-Parent Linkages and Technological Capability-building in TNC Subsidiaries: The Electronics Industry in Malaysia,' in K.S. Jomo and G. Felker (eds.), *Malaysia's Industrial Technology Development: Political Economy, Policies and Institutions*, Oxford: Cambridge University Press, pp. 150–190.

Arnold, E., Bell, M., Bessant, J., and Brimble, P. (December 2000). 'Enhancing Policy and Institutional Support for Industrial Technology Development in Thailand, Volume 1: The Overall Policy Framework and the Development of the Industrial Innovation System,' World Bank, Washington, DC.

Bell, M. and Pavitt, K. (1995). 'The Development of Technological Capabilities,' in I. Haque (ed.), *Trade, Technology and International Competitiveness*, Washington, DC: World Bank, pp. 67–101.

Bell, M. and Scott-Kemmis, D. (1985). 'Technological Capacity and Technical Change,' Draft Working Paper No. 1, 2, 4 and 6, Report on Technology Transfer in Manufacturing Industry in Thailand, Science Policy Research Unit, University of Sussex, Brighton, UK.

Brimble, P. and Doner, R. (2006). 'University-Industry Linkages and Economic Development: The Case of Thailand,' *World Development* 35(6): 1021–1036.

Brooker Group. (2002). 'International Competitiveness of Asian Economies: A Cross-Country Study – Thailand Paper,' Report for the Asian Development Bank, Bangkok: Brooker Group.

Chairatana, P. (1997). 'Latecomer Catch-up Strategies in the Semiconductor Business: The Case of Alphatec Group of Thailand and Anam Group of Korea,' MSc Thesis, SPRU, University of Sussex, UK.

Chang, H. (1994). *The Political Economic of Industrial Policy*, London: Macmillan.

Chang, H. (1997). 'Institutional Structure and Economic Performance: Some Theoretical and Policy Lessons From the Experience of the Republic of Korea,' *Asia Pacific Development Journal* 4(1): 39–56.

Chantramonklasri, N. (1985). 'Technological Responses to Rising Energy Prices: A Study of Technological Capability and Technological Change Efforts in Energy-Intensive Manufacturing Industries in Thailand,' Unpublished D.Phil. Thesis, Science Policy Research Unit, University of Sussex, Brighton.

Charoenporn, P. (2001). 'Automotive Part Procurement System in Thailand: A Comparison of American and Japanese Companies,' Unpublished Master's Thesis, Faculty of Economics, Thammasat University, Bangkok, Thailand.

Cohen, W.M., Goto, A., Nagata, A., Nelson, R., and Walsh, J. (2002). 'R&D Spillovers, Patents and the Incentives to Innovate in Japan and the United States,' *Research Policy* 31(8): 1349–1367.

College of Management, Mahidol University. (2003). 'S&T Needs and Production of Manpower in the Manufacturing Sector,' Final Report Submitted to National Science and Technology Development Agency, Thailand, June (in Thai).

College of Management, Mahidol University. (2006). 'Assessment of Technological and Innovative Capability of Strategic Cluster (Automotive),' Final Report Submitted to the National Science and Technology Development Agency, July (in Thai).

Dahlman, C. and Brimble, P. (April 1990). 'Technology Strategy and Policy for Industrial Competitiveness: A Case Study of Thailand,' Paper Prepared for the World Bank, World Bank, Bangkok.

Department of Intellectual Property (DIP). (2006). 'Information for Thailand's Intellectual Property Right,' Accessed October 7, 2016 from www.ipthailand.org/en/index.php?option=com_content&task=category&sectionid=6&id=57&Itemid=52.

Doner, R. (1992). 'Politics and the Growth of Local Capital in Southeast Asia: Auto Industries in the Philippines and Thailand,' in R. McVey (ed.), *Southeast Asian Capitalists*, Southeast Asia Program (SEAP), New York: Cornell University Press, pp. 223–256.

Doner, R. (2009). *The Politics of Uneven Development: Thailand's Economic Growth in Comparative Perspective*, Cambridge: Cambridge University Press.

East Asia Analytical Unit. (1995). 'Overseas Chinese Business Networks in Asia,' Department of Foreign Affairs and Trade, Canberra, Australia.

Eichengreen, B., Park, D., and Shin, K. (2013). 'Growth Slowdowns Redux: New Evidence on the Middle-Income Trap,' National Bureau of Economic Research No. 18673. National Bureau of Economic Research, Cambridge, MA.

Electrical and Electronics Institute (EE). (2012). 'Industry Report 2012,' (in Thai). Accessed April 7, 2013 from http://eeiu.thaieei.com/Lists/IUHighlight/view.aspx?Paged=TRUE&PagedPrev=TRUE&p_month=201211&p_ID=277&PageFirstRow=16&&View={230220E0-8919-4549-BB48-BEE494417DAB}.

Felipe, J., Abdon, A., and Kumar, U. (2012). 'Tracking the Middle-income Trap: What Is It, Who Is in It, and Why,' Levy Economics Institute of Bard College Working Paper No. 175, Annandale-on-Hudson, New York, Accessed October 30, 2014 from www.levyinstitute.org/pubs/wp_715.pdf.

Food and Agriculture Organisation of United Nations (FAO). (2016). 'The State of Food and Agriculture 2016,' FAO, Rome, Accessed May 7, 2017 from www.fao.org/3/a-i6030e.pdf.

GEM, Bangkok University and BUSEM. (2012). 'Thailand Report 2012,' Global Entrepreneurship Monitor, Bangkok. Accessed April 29, 2017 from http://summeruniversitythailand.org/pdf/GEM per cent20Thailand per cent202012 per cent20Report.pdf.

Gill, I. and Kharas, H. (2007). *An East Asian Renaissance: Ideas for Economic Growth*, Washington, DC: World Bank.

Goto, A. (1997). 'Cooperative Research in Japanese Manufacturing Industries,' in A. Goto and H. Odagiri (eds.), *Innovation in Japan*, Oxford, UK: Oxford University Press, pp. 256–274.

Goto, A. and Odagiri, H. (1996). *Technology and Industrial Development in Japan: Building Capabilities by Learning, Innovation and Public Policy*, Oxford: Oxford University Press.

Haraguchi, N. (2009). 'Impact of the Global Economic Crisis on the Thai Automotive Industry: From the Perspective of the Interplay Between Shocks and the Industrial Structure,' [Online]. United Nations Industrial Development Organisation, Vienna. Accessed October 27, 2014 from www.unido.org/en/resources/publications/publications-by-type/working-papers.html.

Hobday, M. (1995). *Innovation in East Asia: The Challenge to Japan*, Aldershot: Edward Elgar.

Hobday, M. and Rush, H. (2007). 'Upgrading the Technological Capabilities of Foreign Transnational Subsidiaries in Developing Countries: The Case of Electronics in Thailand,' *Research Policy* 36(9): 1335–1356.

Intarakumnerd, P. (2000). 'Thai Telecommunication Business Groups: An Analysis of the Factors Shaping the Direction of Their Growth Paths,' Unpublished D.Phil. Thesis, Science Policy Research Unit, University of Sussex, Brighton, UK.

Intarakumnerd, P. (2006). 'Thailand's Cluster Initiatives: Successes, Failures and Impacts on National Innovation System,' Paper Presented at International Workshop's Program Industrial Clusters in Asia: Old and New Forms, Lyon, France, November 29–30 and December 1.

Intarakumnerd, P., Chairatana, P., and Chaiyanajit, P. (2016). 'Global Production Networks and Host-site Industrial Upgrading: The Case of the Semiconductor Industry in Thailand,' *Asia Pacific Business Review* 22(2): 289–306.

Intarakumnerd, P., Chairatana, P., and Tangjitpiboon, T. (2002). 'National Innovation System in Less Successful Developing Countries: The Case of Thailand,' *Research Policy* 31(8–9): 1445–1457.

Intarakumnerd, P. and Charoenporn, P. (2010). 'The Roles of IPR Regime on Thailand's Technological Catching-Up,' in Hiroyuki Odagiri, Akira Goto, Atsushi Sunami, and Richard R. Nelson (eds.), *Intellectual Property Rights, Development and Catch-Up: An International Comparative Study*, Oxford: Oxford University Press, pp. 378–411.

Intarakumnerd, P. and Charoenporn, P. (2013). 'The Roles of Intermediaries and the Development of Their Capabilities in Sectoral Innovation Systems: A Case Study of Thailand,' *Asian Journal of Technology Innovation* 21(S2): 99–114.

Intarakumnerd, P. and Gerdsri, N. (2014). 'Implications of Technology Management and Policy on the Development of a Sectoral Innovation System: Lessons Learned Through the Evolution of Thai Automotive Sector,' *International Journal of Innovation and Technology Management* 11(3): 1440009 (19 pages).

Intarakumnerd, P. and Wonglimpiyarat, J. (eds.). (2012). *Towards Effective Financing Innovation in Asia: A Comparative Study of Malaysia, Singapore, Taiwan and Thailand*, Bangkok: Thammasat University Press, pp. 61–160.

Jimenez, E., Nguyen, V., and Patrinos, H.A. (2012). 'Stuck in the Middle? Human Capital Development and Economic Growth in Malaysia and Thailand,' World Bank Policy Research Working Paper No. 6283, World Bank, Washington, DC.

Jitsuchon, S. (2012). 'Thailand in a Middle-Income Trap,' *TDRI Quarterly Review* 27(2): 13–20.

Johnson, C. (1982). *MITI and the Japanese Miracle: The Growth of Industrial Policy, 1925–1975*, CA: Stanford University Press.

Kim, L. (1993). 'National System of Industrial Innovation: Dynamics of Capability Building in Korea,' in R. Nelson (ed.), *National Innovation System*, Oxford: Oxford University Press, pp. 357–383.

Kim, L. (1997). *Imitation to Innovation: The Dynamics of Korea's Technological Learning*, Cambridge, MA: Harvard Business School Press.

Kohpaiboon, A. (2009). 'Global Integration of Thai Automotive Industry,' Discussion Paper Series, No. 16, Faculty of Economics, Thammasat University, Bangkok. Accessed September 9, 2017 from www.econ.tu.ac.th/oldweb/doc/content/569/Discussion_Paper_NO.16.pdf.

Kuanpoth, J. (2006). 'TRIPS-Plus Intellectual Property Rules: Impact on Thailand's Public Health,' *Journal of World Intellectual Property* 9(5): 573–591.

Kunio, Y. (1988). *The Rise of Ersatz Capitalism in South East Asia*, New York: Oxford University Press.

Lall, S. (1996). *Learning From the Asian Tigers: Studies in Technology and Industrial Policy*, London: Macmillan Press.

Lall, S. (1998). 'Thailand's Manufacturing Competitiveness: A Preliminary Overview,' Unpublished Paper for Conference on Thailand's Dynamic Economic Recovery and Competitiveness, Session 4, Bangkok, May 20–21.

Laothamatas, A. (1992). *Business Associations and the New Political Economy of Thailand: From Bureaucratic Polity to Liberal Corporatism*, Boulder: Westview Press.

Lauridsen, L. (1999). 'Policies and Institutions of Industrial Deepening and Upgrading in Taiwan III-Technological Upgrading,' International Development Studies Working Paper No. 13, Roskilde University, Roskilde, Denmark.

Lauridsen, L. (June 2002). 'Coping With the Triple Challenge of Globalisation, Liberalisation and Crisis: The Role of Industrial Technology Policies and Technology Institutions in Thailand,' *The European Journal of Development Research* 14(1): 101–125.

Lauridsen, L. (2008). 'Industrial Upgrading: Industrial Technology Policy in Taiwan,' in L. Lauridsen (ed.), *State, Institutions and Industrial Development: Industrial Deepening and Upgrading Policies in Taiwan and Thailand Compared*, Aachen: Shaker Verlag, pp. 442–513.

Levin, R., Klevorick, A., Nelson, R., and Winter, S. (1987). 'Appropriating the Returns to Industrial R and D,' *Brookings Papers on Economic Activity* 18(3): 783–831.

Liefner, I. and Schiller, D. (2008). 'Academic Capabilities in Developing Countries – A Conceptual Framework With Empirical Illustrations From Thailand,' *Research Policy* 37(2): 276–293.

Lin, J. (2012). 'From Flying Geese to Leading Dragons: New Opportunities and Strategies for Structural Transformation in Developing Countries,' *Global Policy* 3(4): 397–409.

Lin, J. and Treichel, V. (2012). 'Learning From China's Rise to Escape the Middle-Income Trap: A New Structural Economics Approach to Latin America,' World Bank Policy Research Working Paper No. 6165, World Bank, Washington, DC.

Liu, M. and Wen, F. (2012). 'Innovation Financing Schemes of Taiwan,' in P. Intarakumnerd and J. Wonglimpiyarat (eds.), *Towards Effective Financing Innovation in Asia: A Comparative Study of Malaysia, Singapore, Taiwan and Thailand.* Bangkok: Thammasat University Press, pp. 61–160.

Malerba, F. (2002). 'Sectoral Systems of Innovation and Production,' *Research Policy* 31(2): 247–264.

Mani, S. (2004). 'Financing of Innovation: A Survey of Various Institutional Mechanisms in Malaysia and Singapore,' *Journal of Technology Innovation* 12(2): 185–208.

Marin, A. and Bell, M. (May 2006). 'Technology Spillovers From Foreign Direct Investment (FDI): An Exploration of the Active Role of MNC Subsidiaries in the Case of Argentina in the 1990s,' *Journal of Development Studies* 42(4): 678–697.

Ministry of Education, Culture, Sports, Science, and Technology (MEXT). (2002). 'Cluster: Cooperative Link of Unique Science and Technology for Economy Revitalisation,' A Published Paper Prepared by Ministry of Education, Culture, Sports, Science and Technology, Tokyo, Japan.

Mukdapitak, Y. (1994). 'The Technology Strategies of Thai Firms,' Unpublished D.Phil. Thesis, Science Policy Research Unit, University of Sussex, Brighton, UK.

National Economic and Social Development Board (NESDB). (January 26, 2007a). 'National Productivity Enhancement Plan,' Unpublished Power Point Presentation.

National Economic and Social Development Board (NESDB). (July 2007b). 'The Growth Potentials of Targeted Industries in the Next Five Years (2007–2011),' Unpublished Power Point Presentation, Bangkok, Thailand.

National Science and Technology Development Agency (NSTDA). (2006). 'Science and Technology Profile 2006,' Bangkok, Thailand (in Thai).

National Science and Technology Development Agency. (2015). 'Annual Report B. E. 2558,' Bangkok, Thailand (in Thai). Accessed March 27, 2017 from http:// waa.inter.nstda.or.th/stks/pub/2016/20160603-nstda-annual-report-2558-final. pdf.

National Science and Technology Policy Committee. (2006). 'Evaluation Report of Activities Under Science and Technology Strategic Plan 2004–2013,' National Science and Technology Development Agency (NSTDA), Bangkok.

Natsuda, K. and Thoburn, J. (2013). 'Industrial Policy and the Development of the Automotive Industry in Thailand,' *Journal of the Asia Pacific Economy* 18(3): 413–437.

Niosi, J., Saviotti, P., Bellon, B., and Crow, M. (1993). 'National Systems of Innovation: In Search of a Workable Concept,' *Technology in Society* 15(2): 207–227.

Odagiri, H. and Goto, A. (1993). 'The Japanese System of Innovation: Past, Present and Future,' in R.R. Nelson (ed.), *National Innovation Systems: A Comparative Analysis*, Oxford, UK: Oxford University Press, pp. 76–114.

Office of Higher Education Commission. (2006). 'Report on Higher Education Development Project,' Ministry of Education, Bangkok (in Thai).

Ohno, K. (2009). 'Avoiding the Middle Income Trap: Renovating Industrial Policy Formulation in Vietnam,' *ASEAN Economic Bulletin* 26(1): 25–43.

Organisation for Economic Cooperation and Development (OECD). (2011). 'Thailand: Key Issues and Policies,' OECD Studies on SMEs and Entrepreneurship, OECD, Paris.

Patel, P. and Pavitt, K. (2000). 'National Systems of Innovation Under Strain: The Internationalisation of Corporate R&D,' in R. Barrell, G. Mason, and M. O'Mahony (eds.), *Productivity, Innovation and Economic Performance*, Cambridge: Cambridge University Press, pp. 217–235.

Paus, E. (2012). 'Confronting the Middle Income Trap: Insights From Small Latecomers,' *Studies in Comparative International Development* 47(2): 115–138.

Phongpaichit, P. and Baker, C. (1995). *Thailand: Economy and Politics*, Kuala Lumpur: Oxford University Press.

Phongpaichit, P. and Baker, C. (1997a). *Thailand: Economy and Politics*, Singapore: Oxford University Press.

Phongpaichit, P. and Baker, C. (1997b). 'Power in Transition: Thailand in 1990's,' in K. Hewison (ed.), *Political Change in Thailand*, London: Routledge, pp. 21–41.

Phongpaichit, P. and Baker, C. (2005). *A History of Thailand*, New York: Cambridge University Press.

Phongpaichit, P. and Baker, C. (2014). 'A Short Account of the Rise and Fall of the Thai Technocracy,' *Southeast Asian Studies* 3(2): 283–298.

Ritchie, B. (2010). *Systemic Vulnerability and Sustainable Economic Growth: Skills and Upgrading in Southeast Asia*, New York: Edward Elgar.

Samudavanija, C. (1990). 'Thailand: A Stable Semi-Democracy,' in Larry Diamond, Juan Linz, and Seymour Martin Lipset (eds.), *Politics in Developing Countries: Comparing Experiences With Democracy*, Boulder: Lynne Rienner, pp. 271–312.

Scheela, W.J. and Jittrapanun, T. (December 2010). 'Do Business Angels Add Value in an Emerging Asian Economy?' A Paper Presented at the Academy of International Business Southeast Regional Conference, Ho Chi Minh City, Viet Nam.

Schiller, D. (2006). 'The Potential to Upgrade Thai Innovation System By University-industry Linkages,' *Asian Journal of Technology Innovation* 14(2): 67–92.

Schiller, D. and Brimble, P. (2009). 'Capacity Building for University-Industry Linkages in Developing Countries: The Case of the Thai Higher Education Development Project,' *Science, Technology & Society* 14(1): 59–92.

Sripaipan, C., Vanichseni, S., and Mukdapitak, Y. (1999). 'Technological Innovation Policy of Thailand,' (Thai version), National Science and Technology Development Agency, Bangkok.

Suchinai, H. (February 15, 2017). '"New Chapter of Investment Promotion" A Presentation Given by Mrs. Hirunya Suchinai,' Secretary General, Board of Investment, Bangkok, Thailand. Accessed March 5, 2017 from www.boi.go.th/upload/ New per cent20Chapter per cent20of per cent20Investment per cent20Promotion_EN per cent20by per cent20Hirunya per cent20Suchinai_1234343.pdf.

Suehiro, A. (1992). 'Capitalist Development in Post-War Thailand: Commercial Bankers, Industrial Elite, and Agribusiness Groups,' in R. McVey (ed.), *Southeast Asian Capitalists*, New York: Cornell University Press, pp. 35–64.

Suehiro, A. (1993). 'Family Business Reassessed: Corporate Structure and Late-starting Industrialisation in Thailand,' *Developing Economies* 41(4): 378–407.

Sutthijakra, S. and Intarakumnerd, P. (2015). 'Role and Capabilities of Intermediaries in University – Industry Linkages: A Case of Hard Disk Drive Industry in Thailand,' *Science, Technology and Society* 20(2): 182–203.

Tanticharoen, M., Flegel, T., Meerod, W., Grudloyma, U., and Pisamai, N. (2008). 'Aquacultural Biotechnology in Thailand: The Case of the Shrimp Industry,' *International Journal of Biotechnology* 10(6): 588–603.

Techakanont, K. (2002). 'A Study on Inter-Firm Technology Transfer in the Thai Automotive Industry,' Unpublished Ph.D. Dissertation, Hiroshima University, Hiroshima, Japan.

Techakanont, K. and Terdudomtham, T. (2004). 'Evolution of Inter-firm Technology Transfer and Technological Capability Formation of Local Parts Firms in the Thai Automobile Industry,' *Asian Journal of Technology Innovation* 12(2): 151–183.

Thailand Development Research Institute. (August 2004). 'Human Resource Development for Competitiveness in Industry,' A Final Report Submitted to National Economic and Social Development Board, Thailand Development Research Institute, Bangkok (in Thai).

Thiruchelvam, K., Chandran, V.G.R., Ng, B.-K., Wong, C.-Y., Sam, C.K. (2012). 'Financing Innovation: The Experience of Malaysia,' in P. Intarakumnerd and J. Wonglimpiyarat (eds.), *Towards Effective Policies for Innovation Financing in Asia*, Bangkok: Thammasat University Press, pp. 161–250.

Tidd, J. and Bessant, J. (2013). *Managing Innovation: Integrating Technological, Market and Organisational Change*, 5th edn, Chichester: Wiley.

Tiralap, A. (1990). 'The Economics of the Process of Technological Change of the Firm: The Case of the Electronics Industry in Thailand,' Unpublished D.Phil. Thesis, Science Policy Research Unit, University of Sussex, Brighton, UK.

Turpin, T., Garrett-Jones, S., and Robertson, P. (June 2002). 'Improving the System of Financial Incentives for Enhancing Thailand's Industrial Technological Capabilities,' Final Report Prepared for the World Bank, World Bank, Washington, DC.

United Nation Conference on Trade and Development (UNCTAD). (2005). 'World Investment Report 2005: Transnational Corporations and Internationalisation of R&D,' UNCTAD, New York and Geneva.

United Nations Industrial Development Organisation (UNIDO). (2006). 'The Role of Intellectual Property Rights in Technology Transfer and Economic Growth: Theory and Evidence,' Working Paper for Strategic Research and Economics Branch, UNIDO, Vienna. Accessed November 8, 2017 from www.viniti.ru/download/russian/INNOV/pubintelprop.pdf.

Virasa, T. (2008). 'University Technology Transfer and Commercialisation in the Emergence of an Innovation-driven Economy: The Case of Mahidol University, Thailand,' A Paper Presented at EUROMOT Conference, Nice, France, 17–19 September.

Warr, P. and Nidhiprabha, B. (1996). *Thailand's Macroeconomic Miracle: Stable Adjustment and Sustained Growth*, Kuala Lumpur: Oxford University Press.

Wong, P. (1999). 'National Innovation Systems for Rapid Technological Catch-up: An Analytical Framework and a Comparative Analysts of Korea, Taiwan, and Singapore,' A Paper Presented at the DRUID's Summer Conference, Rebild, Denmark.

Wong, P. and Singh, A. (2012). 'Innovation Financing Schemes of Singapore,' in P. Intarakumnerd and J. Wonglimpiyarat (eds.), *Towards Effective Financing*

Innovation in Asia: A Comparative Study of Malaysia, Singapore, Taiwan and Thailand, Bangkok, Thailand: Thammasat University Press, pp. 5–60.

World Bank. (1993). *The East Asian Miracle: Economic Growth and Public Policy*, New York: Oxford University Press.

Yusuf, S. and Nabeshima, K. (2009). 'Tiger Economies Under Threat: A Comparative Analysis of Malaysia's Industrial Prospects and Policy Options,' World Bank Publications No. 2680, The World Bank, Washington, DC.

Index

For Product Safety Concerns and Information please contact our EU
representative GPSR@taylorandfrancis.com
Taylor & Francis Verlag GmbH, Kaufingerstraße 24, 80331 München, Germany

www.ingramcontent.com/pod-product-compliance
Ingram Content Group UK Ltd.
Pitfield, Milton Keynes, MK11 3LW, UK
UKHW020945180425
457613UK00019B/537